Elizabeth'

The Sequel to *Darcy Chooses*

A Pride and Prejudice Variation

By
Gianna Thomas

https://www.facebook.com/GiannaThomasAuthor/
https://www.amazon.com/author/giannathomas
http://www.GiannaThomasAuthor.com

Dedication

This book is dedicated with love to my wonderful daughter and to my lovely readers who make my heart glad, with their beautiful reviews. Thank you.

Acknowledgements

If this work proves to be a very good variation of ***Pride and Prejudice***, it is not due to me alone.

There is my Regency editor, #1 Amazon Author, Kay Springsteen, whose help has been invaluable in fine-tuning my writings to make them more interesting as well as more accurate. All Regency authors need to realize that a good Regency editor is worth their weight in gold, and Kay is very valuable in my eyes.

My love and thanks to my lovely daughter who is working with me now that I am an indie author. She is very knowledgeable in so many areas: marketing, website building, Elements. After working for Microsoft for sixteen years, she is extremely tech savvy which I appreciate very much. And an added bonus is that we enjoy working together. We make a great team.

My thanks also to the many authors of P&P variations, what ifs and fan fiction for the help you have given me as a writer and for the joy I've had in reading your books. They have given me hours of pleasure and entertainment that I have never regretted. Keep up the good work!

And, to you my loyal readers, your comments, reviews, and emails are greatly appreciated. I am delighted you have enjoyed my efforts and hope I can do as well or better in the future.

Then, there is a special thank you to the lady who started it all, Jane Austen. Without her wonderful works, particularly ***Pride and Prejudice***, we wouldn't have the delightful plot and beloved characters of Darcy and Elizabeth to read about again and again.

Austen's words are hers, and if I borrow a few from time to time, they will still be her words. No one can say it like Jane Austen.

Table of Contents

Preface

In May of 2016, 'Darcy Chooses – The Complete Novel' was released and did extremely well. Readers seemed pleased with the merging of the prequel 'Darcy and Bingley' and Parts 1 and 2 of 'Darcy Chooses.' The question at that time was 'Should I write a sequel?' Although the book had essentially been wrapped up with the Epilogue, there could be a sequel that would be about the Darcys' honeymoon to Ireland to be published in the Spring of 2017.

Well, that didn't work out because 'Darcy vs Bingley' intruded and demanded to be written first. In April 2017, that book was released and was received as well as 'Darcy Chooses – The Complete Novel.

Now the plan was to have the sequel, 'Elizabeth's Choice,' available in December 2017. However, plans were scrapped again when I got food poisoning the first of August, recuperated for two months, became an indie author during that time as well, and had to republish all my books on Amazon. Ah, the plans of mice, men, and authors. Due to a glitch in Amazon's system, it took a month, when it should have taken about a week, to get the Kindle books up. It took another two months to get the paperbacks also republished.

And, of course, I found that I was not 100% recovered from my illness, almost, but not quite. Very irritating.

But now 'Elizabeth's Choice' is here, and I hope you enjoy it thoroughly. I did more research for this book than I think all the others combined. And it was worth it. Ireland is a beautiful place with a rich heritage, and Darcy and Elizabeth learned quite a bit about it over the month they were there.

So, enjoy the sights and the people the Darcys encounter on their stay. Learn about the famous Book of Kells in Dublin as well as Blarney Castle in Cork. And find out why they went incognito to an Irish pub.

May you enjoy this book and have the wind at your back.
With love,
Gianna Thomas

Foreshadow of Things to Come

Fitzwilliam Darcy grabbed his wife's elbow and pushed her in another direction from where they had been walking. Moving quickly, he steered her into an alley then grasped her hand and quietly ordered her to run.

As they sprinted down the alleyway, he removed his tall beaver hat and tossed it into a rubbish bin behind one of the shops. Elizabeth's mouth dropped open, and she started to question their mad dash but took note of her husband's grim expression and stayed quiet, deciding that William knew what he was about.

Still running, he led them between two buildings, across a street then into another alley. Finding a deep doorway, Darcy pushed Elizabeth into it and whispered, "Trust me, sweetheart." Elizabeth found herself assaulted by her husband's lips and hands, and her eyes got as big as saucers.

"Any idee where they went?"

"No, just keep looking."

The two men who had been searching for them appeared at the end of the alley as William turned slightly to hide his wife from their view. As the men came near, they saw what the couple was doing and guffawed.

"Hey, Benji. Will ye look at that."

The two rough-looking characters continued to snicker and make ribald comments as Darcy began lifting Elizabeth's skirt with one hand as his wife blushed to her toes. With his other hand, he waved the men away while he and Elizabeth ardently hoped they would get the message and leave.

But, they did not.

Chapter I

Elizabeth's chocolate curls lay across the pillow as she slept. With a slight smile, her husband watched in wonder and thought about the night he had just spent with her. He had never realized how lonely he'd been until he met Elizabeth and couldn't believe the joy he felt in seeing her repose. Fitzwilliam Darcy had thanked God before for finding her, and he thanked Him again for his Elizabeth. As his love for his wife swelled his breast, he grinned and placed a gentle kiss on her hair trying not to awaken her. Even so, Elizabeth stirred and opened one eye.

"William?"

"Shhh, go back to sleep, my love."

That turned out to be a useless admonition, and the two were not seen for three days by anyone as they learned more about each other, climbing the heights of passion and plunging together. Darcy was grateful for the discussion he and his cousin Richard had in the Netherfield library concerning his wedding night. But, most of all, he was glad he and Elizabeth had waited and not anticipated their vows. Their wedding night would forever be special to them.

***

Mrs. Reynolds smiled at the laughter coming from the other room as she set the table for the newly married couple. With tears in her eyes, she delighted in the fact her boy was truly happy for the first time in years and that Elizabeth had brought so much joy to Pemberley. Her master had smiled rarely after his father died a little over five years earlier. And after the troubles at Ramsgate, he had been even sterner for far too long.

Darcy had informed Mrs. Reynolds of Wickham's attempted elopement with his sister, Georgiana, so she could watch over her when he had to leave for London. Darcy's sibling had been so melancholy after Wickham's abandonment that he worried about her state of mind. Shy before, she had become even more withdrawn until she made Elizabeth Bennet's acquaintance. Now, everything was changing for the better, and he loved his wife even more for the affection she had shown toward his sister, who was now beginning to blossom into a beautiful, happy young lady.

Mrs. Reynolds looked at Darcy and his sister as her own as she had never had any children after marrying Mr. Reynolds, the Darcys' butler. Lady Ann Darcy nee Fitzwilliam had died in childbirth, when Georgiana was four years old and Darcy sixteen, bringing great sorrow to Gerald Darcy, from which he never recovered. He had endured his grief until he finally succumbed to heart problems, and his son took control of the estate at the young age of only twenty-three.

Darcy took very seriously his responsibilities to the estate and the many servants and tenants who were dependent on his good oversight. Honest, trustworthy to a fault, Darcy worked diligently to keep the estate prospering, and in caring for the many duties for which he had been trained. It was understandable that he was less inclined to smile than most people.

Yet, Elizabeth Darcy nee Bennet had him smiling and laughing, something Mrs. Reynolds had not heard him do in several years. She would be forever beholden to Mrs. Darcy for the wonderful changes she had wrought in Fitzwilliam Darcy. He was like a new man.

The couple had spent three days in the dower house after their wedding and had chosen to see no one except Mrs. Reynolds who had prearranged times for their meals. She would set the table in the connecting parlor to their room then knock on the door to let them know their meal was ready. Quietly and quickly, she would leave the room closing the door behind her, giving them privacy.

***

"Are you hungry, Elizabeth?"

"I am starving, William. I could eat a cow about now, hoofs and all," his wife said with a smile.

He just looked at her, grinned and then gave her a kiss that warmed her to her toes. Although Elizabeth was more than willing to continue with pleasant pursuits, she wasn't willing to eat cold food. Scrambling out of their bed, she quickly dressed while eluding her husband's hands and laughing the whole time. His attempts to catch her were only half-hearted as he had quite an appetite as well. In a few minutes, both were seated at the dressing room's table and partaking of a meal of five delicious items prepared by their housekeeper.

When they were satisfied, at last, both gave a sigh of contentment.

"Where would you like to go on our trip?"

Elizabeth looked up in surprise. "Our trip? I didn't know we were going to take a trip."

Standing and picking up his adorable wife, Darcy set her on his lap and proceeded to kiss her senseless.

"If you keep that up, we will have to go back to the bedroom." She giggled, and he waggled his eyebrows at her.

"We will, but first I need to know where you would like to travel for our honeymoon. I've been thinking about where we could go for about a month."

"A month? But, William, the estate…"

"My steward is already aware that we will be gone for at least a month, and he and I have made arrangements for any contingency. Also, Lord Matlock can help in an emergency."

"Oh. If the estate is being cared for, a trip sounds lovely. Where would you like to go?"

"*Elizabeth*, I asked you first." Darcy could not help smiling at his wife, and she smiled back.

"But, William, I have only been to London and the Lake District. I'm not sure but…perhaps, Bath?"

"I was thinking about traveling a bit farther than just Bath. If it was earlier in the year, we could go to Heather Glen, my estate in Scotland. But it can be rather cold in November, so I thought we might visit Dublin, Ireland—if you wish—for a fortnight then travel on to Cork for the remainder of the trip. There are a number of castles, cathedrals, and other sights for us to enjoy."

Elizabeth grinned and laughed aloud. "I would love to go to Ireland. The Irish brogue has always fascinated me. And I understand the country is beautiful."

"'Tis Ireland then."

"Oh, but will it not take too long to travel from Dublin to Cork?"

"No, my dear. We will travel first a little over a day to Liverpool. I have a Baltimore clipper ship docked there which we will take to Dublin. It is faster than the larger ships, and if we leave early from Liverpool, it will take less than a day to reach Ireland. After our stay in Dublin, we will take the clipper to the Port of Cork, hire a carriage, and continue our travel through the city. I have friends there to whom I would like to introduce you. We will also stay about a fortnight before returning to Liverpool then back to Pemberley."

"It sounds wonderful, William. I have always wanted to travel and see far-away places."

"And I want to show you those places as well. We will finalize arrangements on the morrow and prepare to leave in two days. That will allow me time to contact the captain, so his crew can prepare for our journey. In the meantime, though, I have other plans for today."

"You do?"

Darcy kissed her senseless then said, "Yes, I do." And Elizabeth didn't object at all.

***

The next morning, both arose early, and Darcy told Mrs. Reynolds they were returning to the main house to help prepare for their trip.

The dower house was only about a mile from the Darcys' large home and was a little over a quarter hour walk. Both arrived exhilarated by the exercise and looking forward to leaving in two days.

"Oh, William," exclaimed Elizabeth.

"Are you pleased, my dear?"

"I love the dresses, but…three trunks full of new clothes. How…when…where?"

"The day we went shopping in London for your trousseau, I did some shopping of my own. Do you remember what you did when we went to your uncle's warehouse for fabric?"

"I chose the ones I liked best, and the ones that would complement my skin."

"Did you choose all you liked best?"

"Well…no. There were so many beautiful ones my uncle had just received…and I did not want to appear greedy. Besides, I do not need several wardrobes of clothes."

"Oh, but my darling Elizabeth, as Mrs. Darcy, you do need a larger, in fact, a much larger wardrobe than you would as a gentleman's daughter. Not only will we be entertaining fairly frequently at Pemberley and London when necessary, you need a much warmer one for Derbyshire's frigid winters. We quite frequently receive snow and ice for two to three months most winters. That's why I included two fur-lined coats, fur-lined boots, and gloves as well. Brocade and velvet fabrics have been used for some of your dresses because they will be much warmer. You have several fur hats and muffs also. Have you seen them yet?"

"No, but William, I am overwhelmed. When did all this come about?"

"Come and sit, my love." Darcy gestured to his lap.

When Elizabeth was settled with her head against his chest and his strong arms around her, he continued his story.

"Do you recall when I went back into Mr. Gardiner's warehouse while you and Georgiana waited for me?"

"Mmm…yes. We were so excited about the fabrics, I did not question you at the time and forgot about it later."

"Well, I went back after making note of all the fabrics you had returned to the shelves and told your uncle to put them aside for you. I could not give them to you since we were not married yet, but I could buy them and have the modiste make them up in the latest fashions once she had your measurements. I instructed your uncle to send them to Mrs. Lamont and spoke with her the next day about what I wanted to do regarding your wardrobe. She has also included everything that you will need: morning, day, walking, and tea dresses, plus dinner and evening gowns and all the accessories with...uh any undergarments as well." With this last comment, Darcy blushed bright red as Elizabeth laughed with delight.

"William, we are married now. We can speak of such things, can we not?"

"Elizabeth, I may never be able to speak of some things. I could not with Georgiana, and I'm not sure I can with you either."

"My dear husband, you begin to sound like my father." And she giggled when he huffed at the comparison to Mr. Bennet. "He cannot abide to speak of ribbons and lace and runs to his library when the subject arises with my mother or sisters."

Darcy just sighed and decided he'd rather do something else than speak of family. And he proceeded to kiss his wife most ardently.

About that time, Elizabeth's maid walked in then very hurriedly tip-toed out the door. Neither Darcy nor Elizabeth noticed her entrance or her rapid exit from the room.

***

Later, when Darcy left to attend to business, Elizabeth spent the rest of the afternoon determining which dresses and accessories she would have packed for the trip. To her surprise, Mrs. Lamont had done such an outstanding job with just her measurements, there was little that needed to be altered. Those few dresses would go to the modiste, Mrs. Barkley, in Lambton with whom her husband had made arrangements beforehand.

However, they found they needed an extra day to finish preparations before leaving for Liverpool. Darcy was glad that he had alerted his ship's captain, Robert Lowery, that they might be a day or so later if they were delayed. Captain Lowery was paid handsomely for being at Darcy's beck and call and would reserve several days for their arrival. Darcy had warned him a month in advance that he was getting married and to expect to make a trip to Ireland before winter set in. And Darcy was delighted that his wife looked forward to their Irish adventures as much as he did.

Chapter II

Early on the day of their departure from Pemberley, Elizabeth awoke to her husband ardently kissing her. She could think of no better way to start the day and had found that whether it was late at night or early in the morning, her husband was more than willing to love his beautiful wife. However, she was surprised the day before to find that the middle of the day was most satisfactory as well.

So, this particular morning saw a bit of a delay before the master and mistress of Pemberley arose, dressed, broke their fast, and prepared to leave on the first leg of their trip to Liverpool. All their bags and trunks had been packed the day before, and Darcy had met with his steward for the last time before their departure. Two carriages were being utilized, mainly for the luggage. However, the Darcys had given his valet and her lady's maid leave for the month to visit their families. The new husband and wife were finding that they liked helping the other dress and vice versa, and the hotels would have valets and maids for their convenience once they reached Ireland.

Darcy also hired outriders—as he always did—for the journey to Liverpool. Part of their travel would take them through the Peak District with several places that would be conducive to highwaymen. He would not take any chances that would allow Elizabeth to come to harm. He would always err on the side of safety.

"Sweetheart, if you're getting fatigued, we can stop for the night. The next town has a very nice inn with very comfortable mattresses."

Elizabeth laughed as he waggled his eyebrows at her and smiled. "I am tired and getting a bit of a headache. It seems that I did not get as much sleep last night as I needed."

"Ah, and are you complaining, Mrs. Darcy?"

"No, my darling Mr. Darcy. I am not complaining at all since you have kept me very warm the entire way. I just was not able to get much of a nap."

"It seems I had the same problems as we have been engaged in the same activities for the past week."

"And who is to blame for that?"

"I do believe that both of us are responsible," he growled then took her in his arms and kissed her senseless again much to her pleasure.

"Perhaps we should stop for the night and be early to bed...and early to rise."

"Splendid idea, Mrs. Darcy."

"Yes, I thought you would agree, Mr. Darcy." And she couldn't stop her giggles against his mouth when he kissed her ardently again.

Then, with a sigh, he pulled away, took his walking stick, and tapped the roof of the carriage. His driver called down after stopping the horses, and Darcy told him where they would be staying for the night. He smiled at his wife as the carriage started up again toward their destination. He and Elizabeth both looked forward to an early night.

***

When Darcy and Elizabeth arrived at the inn, they were greeted heartily. Darcy was even greeted by name, showing he was well-known to the proprietor.

"Mr. Darcy, how good to see you. It has been a while."

"Yes, it has been a long while, Duncan. I hope you and your family are doing well."

"We are well. Thank you, sir."

"Things have changed since I was last here. I have married a wonderful woman. May I introduce my wife, Elizabeth Darcy."

"Mrs. Darcy, it is a pleasure to have you stay with us. You have married a fine man."

"Thank you, sir. I agree wholeheartedly." Her eyes strayed toward her husband, and then downward toward the floor, and she felt her cheeks grow warm.

The innkeeper smiled and asked, "How long will you be staying, Mr. Darcy?"

"Only for tonight. Tomorrow we take my clipper ship to Ireland." Looking fondly at Elizabeth, he said, "We are on our honeymoon."

"Oh, then we must at least feed you both well before you depart. Will shepherd's pie, fresh hot bread, our best wine, and an apple tart to end the meal be satisfactory?"

"Elizabeth?"

"It sounds wonderful. I am starving."

Both men laughed, and Darcy agreed with his wife.

"Would you prefer a private dining room or…shall we bring the food to your rooms?" The last was said with a sly look from Duncan as he held back a smile.

Darcy chuckled and replied, "A private dining room is perfect. We will freshen up and be back down in a short while."

Duncan nodded, but the couple missed the wink and smile he gave them as they turned to go upstairs. He was remembering the first few weeks when he married his beloved wife who continued to help him with the inn. With a sigh, he headed to the kitchen to give orders for the special meal for the Darcys.

***

The Inn proved to be rather luxurious for that type of accommodation. It had large bedrooms with roomy double beds, feather mattresses, and expensive accessories. The dressing rooms were larger than most inns and even contained a small water closet for privacy. Elizabeth smiled when she saw the vase full of laurel on the small writing desk and imagined that it would have fresh flowers during warmer weather.

"Oh, William. How lovely this is. It is almost like home."

"Being this close to Liverpool, many of the peerages who will be traveling to other countries would disdain the ordinary inns.

My grandfather hated the inns of his day as being uncomfortable and sometimes not very clean as well. So, he and his two uncles met with Duncan's father and arranged to have this inn built. Although business was slow at first, once Lord Matlock's uncle and grandfather spread the word amongst the *ton* and other of their friends, this has become the only inn in this area where they will stay. To this day, I have my father's share that I receive on a yearly basis."

"Oho, do I find that you are a member of trade, Mr. Darcy?"

"Ah, you found me out, Mrs. Darcy. Do not swoon when you discover that I have numerous investments in trade, including Gardiner's Import-Export. It adds substantially to my income as the business does very well."

"You invest in my uncle's business? My, my, Mr. Darcy, what a secretive man you are."

Both chuckled at her comment. And, as Darcy couldn't resist his Elizabeth's charms, he took her in his arms and gave her a toe-curling kiss.

"Mr. Darcy, if you keep this up, we will miss dinner."

"Yes, my love, I am well aware, however, we have a long journey tomorrow and should eat and then sleep. There will be plenty of time to indulge in more enjoyable pleasures once we reach Ireland. But might I not have a taste of what is to come?"

"Later, beloved. Let's refresh ourselves and go downstairs. You do remember I said I am starving, do you not?"

"Yes." And neither could refrain from laughing as they readied for dinner. Making use of the hot water the maid had brought them, they finished with their ablutions then went downstairs to the private dining room.

When the shepherd's pie and hot bread and wine were brought, Elizabeth blushed as her stomach growled. Both held their laughter until the serving maid left the dining room. As they laughed at what happened, they were unaware that the maid had covered her mouth as she headed toward the kitchen in an effort to stifle her own laughter. It would not have done for her to laugh at one of the owners of the inn.

As they ate the delicious meal, Elizabeth asked about what they would see in Dublin, the first stop on their journey.

"There are a number of places to visit in Dublin. One of them is a surprise, and you will know only when I take you there."

"You will not tell me where? William, you are mean and cruel."

"Never fear, my dear. You will love what Dublin has to offer. One of the places we can tour is Dublin castle. It was founded in 1204 as a defensive measure."

"I look forward to seeing that. I have never been in a castle before."

"As curious as you are, Elizabeth, you will find it fascinating. Another building we can view, but not tour as such, is St. George's church. Two years ago, I saw how much had been constructed, and they still have quite a bit to go before they finish. They began in 1802 and estimated that it would take nigh on close to ten years before the church is completed. I look forward to seeing their progress since I was last there."

"Tell me more."

"I have been debating with myself if I should tell you about this place as it will be an adventure…incognito."

"Incognito? You mean we cannot be ourselves?"

"I mean we will have to dress like lower class persons to go to this place."

"What place, William? You have my curiosity aroused, and you cannot stop now until you tell me of what you speak."

"Would it scare you to be among those of a lower class who might get a little too loud from…perhaps a little too much ale?"

Elizabeth paused and thought about what William had said. "No, I do not think it would scare me if it was not dangerous, just a little noisy."

"That's my lady. When in Dublin, I do not dress as a nabob when I go to Patrick O'Malley's Pub. I dress as a laborer." At

Elizabeth's gasp, Darcy raised his hand and said, "No, no, don't get upset at me dressing so…informally. Those who come to the pub would be uncomfortable with someone of a higher station. Why I wish to take you there is because they have musicians who play, they sing Irish songs all night, and at midnight, they do Irish dancing."

"Would there be room to dance in a pub? I rather thought they might be crowded."

"They are. However, these are single individuals who dance. On the table."

"The table? William, are you sure it would be safe for us to be there?"

Although Darcy chuckled, he understood Elizabeth's trepidation. "Yes, my love, it will be safe. I met Patrick several years ago. He's very strict about patrons in his pub. If they get foxed, they have to leave. If they get rough or pugnacious trying to start a brawl, they can be permanently ousted. If they sing or laugh loudly, no one minds. Everyone has a good time, and Patrick makes them toe the mark. No fighting, no acting badly around the serving maids, hands to themselves."

"And you are sure this…Patrick can keep the peace?"

"Most assuredly. I have been there when one individual tried to start a brawl, and the other patrons ejected him from the pub. They were afraid they might have to leave also if Patrick got too annoyed with their bad manners. Those who come to his pub are friends and know this is a safe place to gather, and they wish to keep it that way. Do you think you could enjoy going there?"

Darcy held his breath as his wife considered. He wasn't sure how adventuresome she would be in an unfamiliar country, but he knew she would enjoy the experience immensely if she agreed to meet Patrick and spend an evening at his pub. The food was good as well as the ale.

"If you say it is safe, I will believe you and go with you." Elizabeth paused and then asked, "How did you meet Mr. O'Malley?"

Darcy's ears went pink as he blushed a little at her inquiry. He sighed and resigned himself to having to tell her that he got careless one day.

"I was there on business with my father and was to meet him for dinner, but...I got lost and found myself in a bad part of town. Two ruffians thought I was a good mark and ran up, one grabbed my horse's reins, and the other grabbed for me. My horse reared and unseated me. One of the men had a knife and raised it just as Patrick threw his dagger and stabbed him in the throat. The other man ran off but was captured later. Patrick saved my life, else I would not be here today. The men's intent was to kill me and steal my valuables. Since then, I've learned to dress in a manner that makes me look...less like a man with lots of money. I have some of those clothes with me in case I need them. I also had your maid pack some of the dresses you wore at Longbourn so you would have something suitable to wear to the pub. However, we will have to shop for some outer garments such as a cloak for you and a coat and hat for me before we go there."

"Why, Mr. Darcy, I had no idea you were such a sneaky sort of man. To think..."

"Don't think, Mrs. Darcy. Just join me on my lap while I kiss you senseless."

Darcy laughed when he saw his lovely wife's eyebrow go up. And Elizabeth couldn't resist laughing either, and sat...on his lap. Neither spoke for the next few minutes as they indulged in a passionate kiss and a bit of nuzzling. Elizabeth had found that she loved it when William kissed her behind her ear and then moved lower to an even better target. But, in a moment, he stopped and gave her another hug and suggested they go to bed and get some sleep. They needed to rise before dawn to ensure they made it to Ireland tomorrow instead of staying another day in Liverpool.

They were interrupted by the serving maid opening the door to the dining room to clear away the dishes. She squeaked when she saw Elizabeth on Darcy's lap and quickly slammed the door as the Darcys burst out laughing.

"Mr. Darcy, we are going to have to be more careful about this."

"I do believe we are, my loveliest, most precious Elizabeth." With that, he kissed her again until both were about to swoon and then released her with a sigh. "We really do need to rise early. And we must have sleep, for tomorrow will be a long day."

Elizabeth stood, smiled, and took her husband's hand in hers, and they proceeded toward the stairway. On the way, Darcy stopped at the desk and told the proprietor to assure the serving maid that everything was fine, and that dinner was delicious.

"Thank you, Mr. Darcy. She is one of our best girls."

After bidding goodnight to Duncan, they climbed the stairs, readied for bed, and Elizabeth slept all night in Darcy's arms.

***

It was still dark when both were awakened by a soft knock at the door. Duncan had remembered to have them alerted to the early hour. His top priority would always be to please an owner when they stayed overnight. Darcy called out his thanks letting the one at the door know they were awake. As Darcy lay there with his arms around his wife, endeavoring to shake the last vestiges of Morpheus, he noted that Elizabeth had gone back to sleep. This was surprising to him as Elizabeth always rose early every morning. Apparently, she was more fatigued than he realized. Softly kissing her hair, he laid back down to let her sleep for about an hour more. He would also make sure she slept in the coach as well.

Chapter III

Elizabeth was a little dismayed that Darcy had let her oversleep, but he assured her that it posed no problem for them. "We will just arrive a little later in the day but should still arrive before dark."

"You are sure I have not delayed us?"

"I am sure, my love. You seemed quite fatigued last night, and I was glad you got a little extra sleep. And you will be able to nap before we arrive at Liverpool."

"But the coachmen and the outriders had to arise so early."

"Do not be distressed, Elizabeth. They make it a point to go to sleep earlier in the evening, knowing they may or may not have to leave at dawn. They travel with Georgiana and me quite frequently, and my sister tires easily riding in a coach for several hours. There have been a number of occasions when I have let her sleep an hour or more so she doesn't arrive exhausted. The men are used to this."

"If you are sure…"

"I am sure. And you look lovely this morning."

With a smile, Elizabeth replied, "And so do you, Mr…."

Elizabeth didn't finish her comment as Mr. Darcy was indulging in one of his favorite pastimes…kissing his wife good morning. It seemed that they would be more than a little late for breakfast.

***

"Mr. Kyle, are you and your men ready?"

"Yes, sir, Mr. Darcy. We…are ready." Mr. Kyle nearly smiled as he remembered that Mr. and Mrs. Darcy were newly married and that some lovemaking in the early hours was not beyond the pale. It wouldn't do to mention they had been ready for three hours, and that the sun had fully risen.

Darcy frowned and shook his head and wondered why his coachman's comment sounded a bit odd. *It must be just my imagination.* So, he thought no more about it. And Mr. Kyle silently breathed a sigh of relief.

After seeing that their trunks were loaded onto the carriage, Darcy went back to get his wife but was surprised that she was nearly to the front door of the inn.

"I hurried to get ready, so I wouldn't delay us any further."

Darcy smiled and assured her, in a quiet voice, that any delay had been thoroughly enjoyed and time well spent as Elizabeth blushed a pretty pink. When she took his arm, he snugged her close and took her to their carriage where he helped her to ascend. Once she was settled facing forward, he joined her on the same seat and closed all the curtains. Tapping the roof with his walking stick, they felt the carriage lurch forward then settle into a steady rhythm.

Mr. Kyle paid strict attention to the horses as they moved into a canter, but he had a smile on his face as he did so. Inside the carriage, Darcy wondered why a couple of the six outriders had laughed aloud after he had closed the curtains. But he didn't dwell on it when he had Elizabeth by his side. For the remainder of the trip, he was more than happy to hold his beautiful wife close as she napped before their arrival.

***

By the time they arrived at Liverpool, it was raining profusely. The leaden sky that they had awoken to had finally released its burden, but they managed to reach town before the road had become dangerous. Tapping the roof, Darcy ordered Kyle to take them to the Kingsley Hotel when his driver stopped to listen. He and Elizabeth would not be leaving for Dublin today.

"Where will Mr. Kyle and the others be staying, William?" Elizabeth's question came about when she noted that the outriders attended by the coach had headed elsewhere after unloading their trunks.

"The Kingsley has a hostel for the men with a large stable for care of the horses. They have stayed there before on earlier trips and have praised the cook and the ale. Although it is easier on my pocketbook, the men have found the accommodations more than satisfactory as the Kingsley maintains a fine reputation in this part of the country. I am sure you will enjoy the rooms."

With a smile, Elizabeth replied, "Anywhere will be enjoyable if you are there."

Darcy felt a thrill of excitement as she drew closer to him. Perhaps, the delay wouldn't be so bad after all.

***

After seeing Elizabeth to their room and having their trunks delivered, Darcy left to inform Captain Lowery of their arrival. Standing under the hotel's portico with his umbrella, he debated the wisdom of going as it was still raining without letup, and he smiled when he thought of Elizabeth waiting for him upstairs in their suite. However, after remaining where he was for a few minutes, the rain slowed enough for him to walk the two blocks to a house he had bought two years earlier to accommodate the captain and his crew when in town.

Arriving at the structure, he tapped on the door with his cane until the housekeeper arrived.

"Welcome, Mr. Darcy. I hope you and your family are well."

"Yes, we are very well, thank you, Mrs. Hopkins. And, when I am able, I will introduce you to my wife."

"Ye are recently wed, sir?"

"As of a week ago."

"So, that is why you have such a happy face," she said slyly.

Darcy's blush told her more than he wanted her to know. His housekeeper was rather a bit impertinent, and he had taken umbrage at that when he first hired her and debated the wisdom of keeping her service. But when he became more acquainted with her, he accepted that as just her personality especially when the captain and crew appreciated her hard work and the spirit she showed in spite of their teasing. She gave as good as she experienced. He was also surprised when the thought struck him as to how much she was like Elizabeth and that his wife would probably like Mrs. Hopkins.

He smiled back at her. "I will introduce you to my Elizabeth when the weather moderates. I believe the two of you will get along famously."

Both laughed, then she asked how she could help him.

"I need to speak with Captain Lowery if he is here."

"Sir, he left about an hour ago to check the ship. The wind was quite bad for a short while earlier and he was concerned. Said he would be back soon. Would you like to wait in the parlor and have some tea or coffee?"

"Yes, I would enjoy some hot coffee. Oh, and some of Cook's biscuits if they are available."

Mrs. Hopkins smiled as if she had a secret and assured him that fresh biscuits had just been baked that morning, and she would bring them with his coffee "quick as a wink."

"Thank you. I appreciate it." He shed his greatcoat and hung it near the front door then walked to the parlor and sat down in a comfortable armchair, pleased at how clean everything was kept. Within minutes, the housekeeper, accompanied by the cook, returned with a pot of coffee and a tray with cup and saucer as well as a plate of lemon biscuits.

"Mrs. O'Riley, are these my favorite biscuits?"

"Aye, Mr. Darcy. Ye have the Irishman's luck that I just baked these this mornin'." Cook said with a smile and a wink.

And Darcy laughed, knowing that Lowery had apprised the women of the trip he and Elizabeth would take to Ireland.

With a sigh of contentment, Darcy sat back to enjoy one of his favorite snacks as he waited for Captain Lowery.

***

With a bang, the front door blew open, and a man in oilcloth rushed in as the rain outside increased considerably. Shutting the door with effort, he breathed a sigh of relief, greeted the housekeeper, and apologized for dripping water all over the floor.

"Mr. Darcy is here to see you, Cap'n."

"Very good, Mrs. Hopkins. I was hoping he and his new wife would arrive safely."

"Would ye like some coffee as you join Mr. Darcy?"

"Yes, thank you. And does Cook have some biscuits as well?"

"Ye scamp. Of course, she does. And I'll bring some for ye as Mr. Darcy may not have left any, bein' his favorite."

Lowery laughed and headed to the parlor where he knew Darcy would be.

"Darcy, were you and your wife able to travel without problem, sir?"

Reaching to shake the captain's hand, Darcy replied, "Yes, our trip was fine until we were within an hour of Liverpool. Then the skies opened up. We arrived safely, but I surmise we may be delayed for a day or so until the weather moderates."

"We may, sir. High winds earlier tore one of the small sails, and my men are working to repair it now. We might leave tomorrow if the weather cooperates."

"My wife and I are not in a hurry if we are delayed only a day or two. I would rather travel in safety than take risks in the middle of nowhere."

"Aye, my sentiments as well." The captain paused then looked at Darcy with a smirk and gave him a wink. "And how does it feel to be a prisoner of parson's mousetrap, eh?"

Darcy hrmphed. "I would be a prisoner of my beautiful wife for the rest of my life and be perfectly content."

"Oho, so that's how it is. You found a love match."

Darcy blushed and agreed but looked at the man with a frown when he noted that Lowery sighed and looked sadly at his hands.

"Lowery, are you well?"

The man shook his head, sighed again then told Darcy of when he married, something he had never shared before with his friend and colleague. "My Carly was the fairest of women in our town. All the young bucks would ask her to dance at the assemblies. I never thought she would even spare me a glance, but she did more than that. She said 'yes' when I asked for her hand. I've never been happier. For two years, she was the light of my life." He stopped and stared at the cup in his hands.

Darcy closed his eyes as he knew without asking that Carly had died.

Quietly, with an unnatural shine to his eyes, the captain continued. "I lost her and our baby boy at his birth."

"I am so sorry, Lowery."

"Thank you. Although it's been many years, it still hurts even today." He shook his head. "'Tis why I have never considered to wed again. I never found anyone who could take her place."

Darcy felt his own heart clench at the man's words and knew that if anything happened to Elizabeth, he would never consider marrying anyone else as no one could replace her. Georgiana would inherit Pemberley and then her offspring as the property was not entailed.

"Excuse me for becoming maudlin. Must be the weather."

Darcy just nodded, and the subject turned to the trip to Ireland.

After a short while, they parted after agreeing to see what weather conditions would be like on the morrow. If need be, they would delay for as long as necessary. Darcy put Elizabeth and the crew's safety first and foremost even above the trip.

***

Arriving back at their suite of rooms, Darcy found Elizabeth asleep, curled up under the covers on the large bed. Hanging his greatcoat up to dry, Darcy stripped, warmed himself by the fire, and then joined his wife.

"William, is that you? Mmm, you are warm."

Darcy growled. "It better not be anybody else." Elizabeth's eyes were still closed as she chuckled, and he began nuzzling her neck. "I feared, as chilled as I was from walking in the rain, that you might not appreciate a cold body snuggling up against you. So, I warmed myself by the fire before joining you."

"Ah, you are a wise man, my husband. Elsewise, you might have seen me leap from the bed in consternation as you placed your cold feet on me. As it is, you feel wonderfully warm."

Darcy smiled and proceeded to heat things up even more for the rest of the afternoon.

Chapter IV

Awakening the next morning, the Darcys discovered the rain had stopped, but the skies were still laden with moisture.

"Are you hungry, Elizabeth? Should we dress and order breakfast?"

"Do you think it will start raining again?"

"This is England, my dear. It can always start raining again."

Both chuckled but remained in bed as the fire hadn't been lit. Darcy had hesitated to have a chambermaid come in early to light the fire for obvious reasons. At Pemberley, the servants had orders not to disturb the newly married couple until they rang for them. It appeared that Darcy would have to light the fire himself, and with a groan, he leaped out of bed and quickly grabbed his quilted robe and slippers.

"It feels like it is freezing in here. I will hurry with the fire."

"There is no rush as I am warm as toast." Elizabeth giggled, and Darcy let out a scandalous chuckle.

"And what if I strip the covers off you, Mrs. Darcy?"

Elizabeth squealed and cried out, "You would not dare…would you, Mr. Darcy?" as she pulled the blankets over her head.

He knelt on the edge of the bed and pulled the covers down and exposed her head. "Oh, wouldn't I, my dear," he said with a leer and waggled his eyebrows. And his wife squealed again and hid her face.

This time he pulled the covers down and thoroughly kissed his wife. "I love you, Mrs. Darcy."

When she could breathe, Elizabeth returned the sentiment then urged him to light the fire, and she snuggled under the covers again. Once it was going strong, he asked her again if she was hungry.

"Yes, I really am. Might we eat in our room rather than the dining room downstairs?"

"Of course. And if it refrains from raining again, we can go see the Pride of Pemberley."

"That is the name of the ship?"

"Yes, and you will love her. She is sleek and beautiful, and she will take us quickly to Ireland, faster than the larger ships. She does fourteen knots when she is in full sail. And if we are lucky, we shall see some of the marine life as well."

"Do you think we might see a whale? I have read about them and have seen drawings also. They are among the biggest animals in the world. Have you ever seen one?"

"Only once, and that one was a humpback. It was a very large whale, and the species is known to make strange noises. It is theorized that they are communicating with other whales of their species that are great distances away."

"They are talking?" Elizabeth's eyes widened as she startled at the thought.

"Actually, they call them whale songs though they are unlike any of the songs we are familiar with."

"I do hope we see one. That would be a tale to tell my father."

"Yes, he would enjoy that. Now, though, we need to order breakfast. What is your desire?"

Noticing the gleam in his wife's eyes and the smile on her face, he waved his finger at her and said, "Oh, no. We will be here for at least another day, and we have plenty of time for that *after* we see the ship and make arrangements to leave on the morrow. The room is almost warm, and I am going to ring for the maid and order breakfast while you get dressed."

He chuckled as Elizabeth stuck her lower lip out and pouted then she laughed aloud and acquiesced by climbing out of the bed. But she didn't get far as Darcy put his arms around her and kissed her senseless.

"You are mean and cruel in making me wait."

"Ah, but once we see the ship and a little of Liverpool, we will have the rest of the day to do as we wish."

"Then you had best get attired before the maid arrives else you upset her sensibilities. She is liable to swoon when she sees how handsome my husband is, especially when he first wakes up."

"Oh, so you think me handsome."

"Yes…and vain….and…." But she got no further as Darcy caught her and gave her another toe-curling kiss just as there was a knock at the door.

Darcy called out, "Please give me a moment. You arrived more quickly than I anticipated." Sprinting across the room, he dressed as rapidly as possible with trousers, shirt, and frockcoat but just put his slippers back on his feet instead of taking time for stockings and boots.

"My apologies for making you wait. The Kingsley definitely has the best service in town."

The maid demurred and refrained from staring at his neck as he had no cravat. "You wish to order breakfast, sir?"

"Yes, please, for me and my wife." Darcy then gave her an order for coffee, tea, eggs, toast and marmalade, muffins, and several rashers of bacon as well as kippers for himself.

"I'll be back in about a quarter hour, sir."

"Thank you, miss."

Closing the door, he missed the smile on the maid's face but turned to find his wife smirking at him. "William, if you continue to cause the maids to blush, I shall wonder that you are flirting with them."

Darcy's jaw dropped, and he tried to quell his indignation until the twinkle in Elizabeth's eye alerted him to her tease. "My dear, whyever would I flirt with another when I have the most beautiful wife in England." With that pronouncement, he gave her a heated look that caused her heart to melt and a kiss that made her almost wish to skip breakfast for more pleasing activities. Almost.

Against his neck, she breathed softly and said, "If you don't let me get dressed, breakfast will be cold, and we will miss seeing the ship." Both laughed and agreed that they were hungry and would like a hot meal as the room still had a bit of a chill until thoroughly warmed by the fire.

Darcy frowned at the knock on the door wondering how it could be timely and yet untimely enough to nearly be aggravating. With a sigh, he reluctantly released his wife then showed the maids where to place the trays. Taking a moment to say grace and gratitude for the meal after she came from the other room, he squeezed Elizabeth's hand to let her know how grateful he was that she had said 'yes' to his offering for her. He was the happiest man in England as he drank his coffee and Elizabeth sipped her tea, both grateful their liquid refreshments were hot and warming. A half hour later, they were ready to see the ship and make arrangements with Captain Lowery for the trip on the morrow.

***

"Oh, William, she is lovely."

Darcy puffed up with pride that Elizabeth was favorably impressed with the clipper ship. "It is the only one of its kind docked at Liverpool although several others had made stops at the city on the way to other destinations over the last five years. Clipper ships had begun being built around 1770 in America on Chesapeake Bay and appearing shortly after the war with the colonies. They are very fast with low water resistance and speed under sails, with or against the wind."

"She is noticeably smaller than the other ships docked here. Is that part of what contributes to her speed?"

Darcy smiled at his wife and thought *I love this woman. She is not only beautiful, she is intelligent.* "The basic concept for Baltimore clippers came from the Chesapeake schooners that are the mainstay of ship building for the state of Maryland in America. Schooners are 'sharp built' and that means they have a merchant type or fast sailing hull enabling them to be used in carrying small bulk expensive items like tea or spices or used as letter of marque service or for privateering."

"You mean pirating?" Elizabeth's jaw had dropped, and her eyes had gotten rounded like saucers.

"Yes, I mean pirating," said her husband with a smile.

Once she got over her surprise, Elizabeth had another question. "You mentioned a letter...what is that?"

"A letter of marque service from a country allows a ship to engage enemy vessels and take prizes, particularly during a time of war."

Elizabeth shivered. "We are at peace for the moment since Napoleon defeated Prussia last year and the Russians in June. Those have given us a measure of peace on the continent, but I fear it may not be for long. I had hoped 1807 would see permanent peace and relief from Napoleon's efforts."

"Many had hoped the same." He cocked his head to one side and just stared at her for a moment then smiled. "I should have known that you would have kept up with the war news. You are unlike any other woman I have ever met, and I am delighted."

Elizabeth blushed furiously and mumbled something about reading her father's newspapers and discussing the war with him.

"I am pleased that we have even more topics for discussion on a daily basis. There are few things more enjoyable than a good debate." Both laughed as he waggled his eyebrows at her and snugged her close to his side.

Silence reigned only for a moment more before his wife had more questions. "William, why do you have a ship that could be used for nefarious means?"

"My dear, I am an investor in the Chesapeake Bay Shipping Company. I bought this Baltimore clipper hoping to find buyers here in England. Captain Lowery is my representative and finds out the names of owners of the various ships that dock in Liverpool. Then he sends them letters in my name inviting them to sail on the Pride of Pemberley. When requested, I meet with the owners and ensure them that everything is legitimate. Merchants especially are interested so they can import items such as tea from China or coffee and sugar from the Caribbean more swiftly than conventional ships.

As you can see, the clipper will not hold a lot of cargo but is perfect for those small, more expensive items."

"I have noticed that it sits much lower in the water than the larger ships. Is the hull shallower than the other ones?"

"Yes, that eliminates much of the drag giving it greater speed."

"What else makes it different from the larger ships?"

Pleased that his wife was showing such interest in regard to something that gave him great pleasure, Darcy was more than willing to answer any questions she had for the rest of the day.

"Most clipper ships have only two masts but have a very large sail area allowing them to travel more swiftly than larger ships. The Pride does have three masts as this allows Captain Lowery to show the largest clipper to a prospective buyer then to inform him that one with two masts could be ordered if he is reluctant to meet the price. Both are approximately 100 feet in length so overall size is the same. However, a third mast makes available a much larger sail area that will be an advantage either when sailing with the wind or against it. The third mast will also make for a swifter trip which is another reason I purchased this particular vessel. When I travel to my estate in Ireland, I want to spend my time caring for the estate not traveling to get there."

"Another difference is that we carry no figurehead such as the mermaid on the vessel over there."

As Elizabeth looked to the other ships bowsprit, she saw a naked mermaid and blushed a bright red.

"My apologies, my dear. I'm used to seeing these figureheads and should have forewarned you."

"But why is she…."

"Without clothing?"

Elizabeth nodded vigorously.

Darcy knew better than to laugh, so he just launched into the explanation with a straight face. "It is because of superstition, sweetheart. Sailors, for the most part, feel like women are bad luck when on board their ship. They think it causes contention among the sailors and other problems that create situations where the men will neglect their work and perhaps cause accidents or possibly even sink the ship through carelessness. However, rather contrarily, they believe that naked women are said to be a calming element for the sea. Thus, most of the figureheads are without clothing especially on the older ships."

"Oh."

"Do not be embarrassed, Elizabeth. I am pleased that my wife has all the sensibilities of a lady."

Elizabeth just giggled and temporarily hid her face against the sleeve of his greatcoat. She quickly looked up, though, when a man on deck called out to her husband.

"Mr. Darcy, you and your wife please come aboard."

"Good morning, Captain Lowery."

Once they were on deck, Darcy introduced Elizabeth to the captain.

"Elizabeth, this is Captain Lowery, my friend and colleague. Captain, this is my wife, Mrs. Elizabeth Darcy."

The Captain bowed over her hand and said how pleased he was to meet her.

"My pleasure as well, Captain. I look forward to our trip to Ireland. I've never been on a ship before."

"I and my men will do our best to see that you have a pleasant and safe trip, Mrs. Darcy. And congratulations to you and Mr. Darcy on your recent marriage."

"Thank you, sir. I could not have married a more wonderful man."

Darcy stood a little taller and pulled his wife a little closer to his side. Several sailors nearby grinned at one another until the captain raised an eyebrow at them to resume their work. He would allow no levity concerning the owners.

***

After their tour of the ship, Darcy and Elizabeth, along with Captain Lowery, discussed whether travel would be possible the next day. Because this was England and winter was approaching, they decided to adopt a 'wait and see' attitude. They would not try for Ireland if the weather wasn't clear as they wouldn't be able to take advantage of the partial moon should the trip take a full twelve hours. The Darcys were not in such a hurry that they would sacrifice safety over prudence.

As they walked around Liverpool, after viewing a number of the larger ships that were docked there, they had luncheon at a delightful restaurant known for its delicious food. During their meal, they were dismayed when the heavens opened up again, and they had to delay their return to the hotel until the rain abated. And the skies did not clear for two days. However, the Darcys were not worried about their trip to Ireland. They spent the time in debating about their favorite books, the state of politics in England, and in more pleasurable pursuits.

***

"Elizabeth…Elizabeth." Darcy hated to wake his wife, who was sleeping so peacefully, but the day had dawned clear with a beautiful sunrise.

Elizabeth just smiled and snuggled closer to her husband without even opening her eyes.

"Wife, you need to wake up as it looks as if the weather will cooperate for us traveling today."

With those words, his bride opened her eyes, smiled, and gave him a toe-curling kiss that almost made him wish they didn't have to ready themselves to leave. But he wanted to arrive in Dublin today while the weather was favorable. With a sigh, he pulled away then kissed her quickly again and arose from the bed. As he was naked, and the room was cold, he quickly dressed then rang for a maid to order breakfast. While Elizabeth dressed, he built the fire and had it going well by the time the maid arrived. Breakfast would arrive in a quarter hour.

"So, my dear, you laughed at me as I was trying to dress." Darcy gave his wife a mock glare.

"Of course, I did. I had to hold back my laughter when you broke out in goose flesh from the cold. It made your chest stand out a little more than usual. It was also rather appealing."

Darcy couldn't resist her when she teased him, and he enveloped her in his arms and gave her a passionate kiss that left them both breathless.

"Mr. Darcy, I think we should wait if we expect to get to Ireland today," she said with a smile.

With a sigh, he agreed, and they began packing their trunks as they waited for their breakfast to be delivered.

Chapter V

As they left the hotel, Elizabeth inquired, "Shouldn't we have had the trunks sent to the ship?"

"I want to speak with Captain Lowery first and make sure that we will be leaving today. We can always send one of the men with a message to get them to the ship if we are going to depart shortly. The hotel is paid through tomorrow and will apply it to our bill when we return if we do depart in a little while."

"Ah, my husband the man of business has cared for everything. What would your family say about you being in…trade?" she whispered.

Darcy smiled. "Not a thing, my dear, as they are in it with me as well. Uncle Percy and the Viscount have also invested in the clipper ships, and we have done very well so far. I also look forward to speaking with Mr. Gardiner about investing in his business, if he is willing."

"Aha. The truth is out. Mr. Darcy is joining the riff raff in becoming a member of trade. Oh, how ignominious of you."

Both laughed and then hired a hack and continued on to the ship.

Lowery spotted them immediately when they arrived and came to the dock to greet them.

"Good morning, Mr. and Mrs. Darcy. Do you look to traveling today? Conditions do allow for it."

"Very good, Captain. We are anxious to get to Dublin. Can you send one of your men to the hotel to have them deliver our trunks?"

"Yes, sir. We will leave as soon as the trunks arrive. The men have put up the moonraker and skysail as the winds are light and we want to take advantage of all air movement today."

"Capital! I have every confidence we will arrive before dark."

"Captain Lowery, what is a moonraker and a skysail?"

"Mrs. Darcy, they are the two sails above the regular sails on the middle mast. Ordinarily, the top sail is the royal sail, but the moonraker—also called a moonsail—and skysails are smaller sails can be added above the royal in order to make the most of light winds. If you look at that mast, the top sail is the skysail, the moonraker is next, and the royal sail is third from the top with the other larger sails below it. The more canvas exposed to the wind, the greater our speed, as much as fourteen knots. We hope to make Dublin in ten hours."

"So, we leave immediately then?"

"Yes, sir. Food and water have already been put on board. Let me send Jamison to the hotel, and we'll have your trunks hopefully within a quarter hour, and we will leave as soon as they are loaded. You and Mrs. Darcy can stay in my quarters if the water gets too rough."

Darcy laughed and commented, "Captain, I imagine I will have trouble getting my wife *off* the deck. She has a tendency to be a little adventurous, and this is completely new to her. She may be on deck for the entire trip."

Both men laughed as Elizabeth blushed and slapped her husband's arm. "William, you know I love learning about new things. Of course, I will be on deck most of the time. I hope to see a whale."

Several of the sailors nearby had heard Darcy's comments and just shook their heads. Some were a little nervous having a woman on board and were muttering under their breaths.

"Well, Mrs. Darcy, I do hope we see a whale for your sake." The captain refrained from mentioning that most of the trip would consist of just endless water with possibly no sightings of the marine life found there.

***

Things went as Captain Lowery said. The trunks arrived quickly, and the ship got underway before a much larger merchant ship was ready to sail. That was fortunate as they would have lost a half-hour to an hour's time waiting for the larger ship to sail out of their way.

Elizabeth was mesmerized as she watched the sailors maneuver the ship until they were completely free of the docks and other vessels and headed to Ireland. All were thankful the skies remained clear and the sun was rising high in the sky. Mrs. Darcy's only complaint was that the wind was colder than she expected. But true to her nature, she stayed on deck doing her best to miss nothing of this new adventure.

Four hours into their voyage, the water all around the ship became agitated and suddenly a large pod of dolphins appeared. "Bloody hell, there must be a thousand of these critters. Uh, sorry, ma'am."

Elizabeth, though, was too captivated by a sight that many sailors had never seen to have taken umbrage at the sailor's words.

"William, what are they, and why are they swimming across the front of the ship?"

"They are dolphins, and they love swimming across the bow planes of ships."

"Why would they do that?"

"I do not know if the reason they swim in that manner is really understood. It might be a type of play to them." Darcy started to say something else when Elizabeth gasped as a large dolphin shot up into the air, spun twice and landed with a big splash that sprayed water in her face. Sputtering in shock, she took the large handkerchief Darcy handed her and began drying the water off her skin and hair. Then she smacked her husband's arm that he dared to laugh at her, but she began laughing also.

"Are they a special type of dolphin because they spin?" Elizabeth asked after drying her face and grinning at her husband.

He grinned back. "These are known as bottlenose dolphins and are the main ones seen here in the Irish Sea. And as you saw, they do spin. However, there are dolphins found in warmer waters known as Spinner Dolphins who don't just spin once or twice, but spin six or seven times."

"Why?"

"No one knows, but they can spin six times in the wink of an eye."

"Amazing."

For over an hour, the Darcys and the crew enjoyed the antics of the huge pod of dolphins as they leaped, twisted, and turned in the air before landing with a resounding splash that sent water over ten feet in the air. The crew made estimates of the total number in the pod including one sailor who climbed a mast and endeavored to do a count. Estimates were upwards of a thousand or more. All on the ship were flabbergasted when within seconds there was not a dolphin in sight. And even though they looked far and wide in every direction, they never saw them again.

But all were in awe at what they had seen because that particular scenario might never occur again within sight of this crew. One sailor even approached Elizabeth and apologized to her. "Ma'am, I'm one of them which don't want women on board ship 'cuz I thought they bring bad luck. But you, ma'am, brought us good luck. We seen somethin' good today, and I believe it 'cuz you on board. Thank ye, ma'am."

Before Darcy could stop her, Elizabeth extended her hand to the man and, as he gingerly extended his own, she shook it. "*Thank you*, sir. I appreciate all your hard work and that of the other men for caring for my husband and me this day. And I am delighted that we all have just witnessed a special part of God's creation. Perhaps, we will see more wonders as we travel together as well."

As she said this, she smiled and nodded to the other men who were close by not aware that the sailors who heard her words would tell the others, and by the end of their travels, there would not be a man on board who would not give his life to help the wife of Mr. Darcy. They already respected the owner, and now they respected his wife as well.

Since all the excitement had ended for a while, Elizabeth became aware she was hungry and tired. She and Darcy went below to the Captain's cabin where they found sandwiches, ale, and water.

"Are you well, my darling?"

"Yes, William, I am well. Just a little tired. It was so fascinating to watch the dolphins, and even though it was a wonderful sight, I hope we see a whale before we arrive back at Liverpool. In fact, I wish we could see all the animals found in the ocean. I never knew that being on a ship could be so exhilarating."

Her husband gently laughed and taking his beautiful wife in his arms, he kissed her thoroughly. The insipid women of the *ton* could not hold a candle to this magnificent woman, and he felt blessed.

Urging her to eat and then take a nap, both fell on the meal and were grateful for it. It had been nearly six hours since breaking their fast, and they were famished. A while later, both sat back, sated with food, and Elizabeth was in dire need of a nap unaware that she was eating and sleeping for two.

After seeing her settled in the captain's hammock where she immediately fell asleep, Darcy headed back up top to speak with Lowery and get an estimate of when they would arrive. The captain determined their position and showed Darcy where they were on the map.

"If we are able to maintain our speed, we should arrive in about five hours. That will put us a bit past sunset but should not be a problem as we have enough of the moon visible to help light our way. And, if we are lucky, we will have part of the waning moon for our trip back to Liverpool."

"Very good. I know that your crew is one of the best in England and that we will travel safely."

The captain chuckled. "We have to be as we have a very pernickety owner."

Darcy huffed then laughed and agreed with him. "Yes, I must admit to being very precise and fastidious with everything I do and am associated with. It is the best way I know to make sure things get done." He paused then said, "If you have a few moments, I would be interested in how the meeting went with Sir Michael Talbot."

The baronet had just come into a large legacy and wished to invest part of it to increase his wealth. Lowery had met with Sir Michael and his man of business just a few days earlier.

"Sir Michael and Mr. Jeffers liked the Pride of Pemberley but felt that the investment was more than they should become involved with at this time. Mr. Jeffers did mention that he knew of several others who might be interested, two of them being merchants looking to increase their profits who could benefit from having at least one clipper ship for expensive items like tea and spices. He did question whether or not some of the buyers were also investing in opium from China."

"Did you assure him that we have all the buyers investigated and will not sell to known traffickers of opium?"

"Yes, I did. He was relieved to hear of our restrictions and said he was sure the two merchants were honest men who would not consider the opium trade. So, I encouraged him to speak with them and send me word if they were interested."

"Excellent. As soon as you discover who they are, express their names and locations so I can let my investigators know. If they purchase, I will see that you get a nice bonus."

"Very good. It's always a pleasure doing business with you, Mr. Darcy."

William and Lowery had been friends and business associates for three years, and although he was Darcy in private, Lowery was always careful to call him Mr. Darcy when around the sailors. It would never do to let them know that when it was just the two of them that their social sphere was no hindrance. The only other person Darcy had a similar relationship with was Charles Bingley.

***

Elizabeth awoke the latter part of the afternoon ending a three and a half-hour nap. Feeling refreshed, she hastened up to the deck to find her husband and hoping she had not missed any of the fascinating marine life.

Darcy spotted her immediately as she appeared from below, and with great strides, he appeared at her side much to her relief.

"I couldn't see you at first and began to worry…just a little."

"My darling, please know that I will never be far from your side if I can help it. And it has been very quiet…too quiet since you stayed below. Did you have a good nap?"

"Yes, I feel quite well. To sleep a bit has done wonders for me. I feel like a new woman."

"Oh, but you must not change, my dear, because I love you as you are."

Elizabeth blushed prettily and looked at her feet as her husband gazed at her with love. Both were so enamored with each other, they failed to notice the smiles on several of the nearby sailors. However, Captain Lowery saw their expressions and made a mental note to caution his men concerning the newly married couple after they were in the Port of Dublin. He had taken note of some of the sailors' comments concerning the Darcys when they went below for lunch and was pleased the men were favorable toward them, but he would not tolerate any disrespectful expressions, verbal or otherwise. Intimate talk among his crew was common but involved the lightskirts of whichever port they found themselves in. All the men were single, so there were no wives to complain when their husbands would be traveling and gone for weeks at a time. Conversation could become rather ribald, and Lowery didn't want the Darcys to find themselves the topic of shipboard gossip. He had already cautioned two of his men when one had uttered a double entendre that Mr. Darcy could have taken great umbrage over if he had heard it. Lowery would not have his friend and his wife become objects for jesting.

"William, did I miss anything while I slept?"

"Not really, my love. We have seen a few sea birds, and they have been our only sightings."

He smiled when Elizabeth sighed in relief. She hadn't missed seeing a whale. What she would get to see would be her first sunset out on the Irish Sea.

Elizabeth was dismayed when she noted how low the sun was on the horizon. "Oh, I thought I just slept for a short while. How long did I nap?"

"For close to four hours. I checked twice to make sure you were well but decided not to disturb you."

"I didn't mean to sleep so long. I wanted to watch for whales before we arrived at Dublin."

"Never fear, I would have awakened you if we had seen any other sea creatures. I know you would have my head on a platter if you missed such a spectacular sight."

Both laughed as they pictured his head in such a position, and William drew his wife closer to his side with a quiet sigh, wishing they were already docked and at their hotel for the night and alone. He would have been pleased to know that his wife felt the same way.

***

A short while later, Lowery handed Darcy a spyglass and pointed out the Poolbeg Lighthouse. "We've made good time and should reach Dublin in about an hour. The crew is already tacking so we will be a little north of the lighthouse. We should spot the other lighthouse soon, and we will sail between the two until we reach the Port of Dublin. I surmise we appear to be in luck as there seems no trace of fog tonight."

"That relieves my mind. When I recall the one time the fog rolled in as we docked, I shudder at the memory."

"Was it very bad, William?"

"The fog was so heavy that night, we could barely see twenty feet in front of us. If we hadn't already arrived, we very easily could have hit the rocks or destroyed the ship on the cliffs."

"Never fear, Mrs. Darcy, if fog should appear, we will drop anchor and wait for it to dissipate."

Elizabeth sagged against her husband's side relieved that the captain had a contingency plan if necessary. Darcy held her close and frowned a little as he contemplated why his intrepid, spunky wife seemed a little daunted. Determined to be watchful in case she was becoming ill, he held his tongue. He was grateful she hadn't experienced seasickness as many people had when on a ship, but he was just a little worried that something might be happening to unsettle his darling wife. He would do whatever was necessary to protect her from any threat, as she was too precious for him to lose.

Chapter VI

Elizabeth smiled at the lovely sunset. There were just enough clouds to the west to light up the sky with orange, yellow and reds until the sky was brilliant with color.

"William, have you ever seen a lovelier sunset?"

"Never, my love. Having you with me makes all the difference in the world. Everything appears so much more beautiful. But not as beautiful as the woman by my side." He snugged her just a little closer as he uttered words that made her blush and her heart swell with the love she had for him. And she could feel a pricking at the back of her eyes as she endeavored to control the emotions that his words summoned up.

Turning into his coat, she quietly uttered, "I love you, William," and was comforted when he drew her a little closer than society would deem proper. Neither was embarrassed that there were dozens of sailors on board who could see them. For that moment, there was only the two of them.

**

Heading down the channel to the port of Dublin, all on board could see lights appearing in various buildings along the way as candles were lit for the evening. As they got closer to the port, they could see the larger flares of torches lighting the docks where all the ships were gathered. Some were still being unloaded, and the sailors rushed to get done with their work, so they would have the evening free for meals and entertainment while in port.

"William, why are the ships so much smaller than the ones we saw in Liverpool?"

"The channel is too shallow to allow the larger ships to come in. If a large merchant ship arrives, it anchors outside the channel and smaller ships bring the cargo into the docks."

"That would mean a lot of extra work, I would think."

"Yes, it does, and there have been meetings with port authorities and other interested parties who gather from time to time to determine if there is a solution to the problem. One that has been offered is to deepen the channel, so it could be utilized by larger ships including some of the war ships. However, that would be a huge undertaking, and it would be years before it would be finished. But no decision has been made, and business continues to be conducted in this manner. It will be more years, I daresay, before an adequate solution is agreed upon."

"It would seem to be a rather complicated situation."

"Quite so, my dear."

Seeing that the Darcys were speaking again instead of snuggling, Captain Lowery approached them. "We should dock in about a quarter hour and soon be able to disembark. I'm pleased that we had good weather and favorable winds the entire trip for you both to enjoy."

"Indeed, Captain. I compliment you and your men on a fine crossing. My wife and I have enjoyed it immensely."

"Agreed. And your lovely wife has endeared herself to the whole crew. The sighting of the dolphins has made them realize that having a genteel lady aboard has been good luck rather than bad. They are willing to carry you both wherever you wish."

"Tell the men I'll stand for an ale for all of them this evening. Advise the pub owner that I will settle the bill with him on the morrow."

"Aye, Mr. Darcy, and you and the missus will have every man of them at your back if you ever need them."

Darcy nodded and held out his hand which Lowery shook with enthusiasm. And those who had traveled with Darcy before smiled as they recognized they would have free ale this evening. However, they would be aware of how much they drank as the owner of Pride of Pemberley was a very pernickety man and would not tolerate the men getting too disorderly and bringing shame on him while in port. In fact, they would be informing the new hires of the rules they would be expected to abide by. So long as they didn't break the law or raise any tavern owners' or Abbess's ire, they were free to do as they pleased until the Darcys were ready to sail to Cork in a fortnight.

**

Once docked, Darcy made arrangements for a carriage to take them to the Dublin West Hotel, the best in town. Several of the men loaded up the Darcys' trunks surprised at how many there were. Unbeknownst to them, the Darcys would be visiting friends and would attend a ball or two while in Ireland and had to be ready for any social occasion. Elizabeth had been shocked when her husband had advised her that two trunks would not suffice. So, the total number they had with them was seven: four were Elizabeth's and three were Darcy's. He would not settle for less, and his wife would learn that there was wisdom in his decision.

When they arrived at the hotel, Elizabeth found that they had a suite of rooms that Darcy had secured well before their arrival. He made sure that he had the biggest and most comfortable suite the hotel offered. Nothing was too good for Mrs. Darcy.

"William, these are beautiful rooms, much more than we need."

"Oh, I disagree, Elizabeth. I want to make love to you in every room."

He smiled as she blushed bright red at his words. Even though she was just as passionate as he, or even a little more so, she still found it a bit embarrassing to actually speak of it. And, yet, she felt her heart begin to race and her body respond as he spoke of making love to her. Especially when he came up behind her and began nibbling on her ear, then her neck.

"Should we wait until we have freshened up and had dinner?" Her last words were lost when her husband gave her a kiss that made her toes curl. Dinner was put on hold.

**

"Yes, and I am a little weary as well. The crossing was wonderful but a bit tiring, even with my nap. And I'm delighted the rooms are warm without me wearing several layers of clothing."

"Shall I warm you some more, my dear?"

Elizabeth gave her smirking husband a little frown. "I do not think so for now. You have warmed me thoroughly, and now I want some food before I sleep. Otherwise, I will be ravenous in the morning."

"Just for food?"

Elizabeth giggled. "No, I will want you first then breakfast. It is a most delicious way to start the morning."

Darcy couldn't resist. He pulled her on his lap and proceeded to kiss her senseless until she lay against his chest, panting.

"William, I really need to eat. I'm not usually this hungry, but my appetite seems to have doubled."

Darcy looked closely at his wife, wondering if she was already carrying his heir. It was too soon though, wasn't it? "Do you feel well, Elizabeth?" the worry showing in his voice.

"Yes, my darling. I am fine. I just need food and rest, especially if we keep busy tomorrow. I promise I have no aches or pains…just yearnings." Elizabeth laughed aloud and jumped off his lap and out of reach of his hands. "Order dinner, please, while I dress."

With a sigh, Darcy obeyed despite having a hunger other than for food. He found he had married a very passionate woman. He had been celibate all his life, but now he had the freedom of a wife who enjoyed intimacy as much as he. And he couldn't get enough.

***

The Darcys found the dinner delicious and praised the hotel to the kitchen maid who came for the dishes. However, Elizabeth found she had eaten just a bit more than was prudent.

"Oh, I feel like a stuffed pig," she moaned. And she frowned at her husband who burst out laughing.

"How dare you, sir, to laugh at me when I am suffering." But she couldn't keep from laughing herself when Darcy laughed even harder.

"You said you were starving, so we ordered food. Now that you have eaten, you are miserable because you ate too much. Wife, will you never be satisfied?"

"Hmph, perhaps not. Then again, there is tomorrow morning." Before turning toward the bedroom, she gave her husband a wink and ran.

Chapter VII

The next morning, the Darcys were late in arising. Although crossing the Irish sea was an enjoyable trip, it had been a bit tiring for the couple. And, after all, they were on their honeymoon and had no obligations of estate or family. This allowed them time to enjoy the peace of having no responsibility for one month. Taking up the reins of estate matters or, in Elizabeth's case, learning to be mistress of Pemberley, one of the largest estates she'd ever seen, were matters left on hold for the moment. The thought of it was still a little daunting, however, knowing that Mrs. Reynolds would enlighten her as to her duties as Mrs. Darcy, Elizabeth felt she would be in good hands. In the meantime, she would cherish her time in Ireland with her husband.

Elizabeth smiled as she looked at her husband across the small dining table. *He's my husband, and the handsomest man I know. And the kindest and most wonderful man I ever met. What did I do to deserve him?*

Darcy looked up at his wife and smiled. "A penny for your thoughts, my love."

"I'm just admiring the wonderful man I married." She laughed as the tips of his ears turned pink. "But 'tis true. I feel very fortunate to have caught your eye."

Reaching across the table, Darcy gave her hand a little squeeze. "I am the fortunate one, Elizabeth, that you said yes when I offered for you. You have made me the happiest of men."

With his hand still resting on hers, Elizabeth raised his hand to her mouth and kissed his fingers, and the hearts of both swelled with love for the other. Never had either been as happy as at that moment.

"What will we see today, William? I find I wish to see all of Dublin while we are here."

Darcy laughed. "My dear Elizabeth, I am afraid that a fortnight would not be long enough to see everything Dublin offers. However, I think you will be pleased with what I believe you will enjoy."

"So…where do we go today?"

"That's a surprise. But…I suppose it is one that we might see more than once while here. There are various aspects to it that demand more time than just one morning."

"Now, sir, you have my interest, however my curiosity demands to know what we will see."

"Ah, now, my dear. It would not be a surprise if I told you where we were going." He couldn't suppress the laughter that bubbled forth when his lovely wife pouted and let her lower lip tremble. And neither could his wife hold her laughter back as well. At his wife's smile, Darcy gave in but only a little and told her they would see Dublin's Trinity College that day but refused to tell her what they would see there. For a fact, he expected her to be astounded at what could be seen.

"Finish breaking your fast and get dressed. We are expected to arrive before noon."

"But, William…."

"I sent a note to my confederate at the college early this morning letting him know we arrived safely in Dublin yesterday. He is looking forward to our visit."

"Very well. I'm looking forward to our visit also. I am nearly done. If you will help me dress, we should be able to leave in a half hour?"

"That would be perfect, my dear."

Within a half hour, the Darcys were walking out the door of the suite and meeting the carriage that would take them to the college. Elizabeth couldn't wait to see William's surprise.

***

As they approached the college, they could see one building that stood out from the others. It was larger than the surrounding structures, and it piqued Elizabeth's curiosity.

58

"What is that building, William?"

"That is the Trinity College Library, and they have large numbers of ancient books."

"Is that where we are going?"

Darcy smiled at Elizabeth's enthusiasm as she nearly bounced on the carriage seat. At this point, he couldn't keep their destination a secret any more. "Yes, that is where we will visit today and, possibly, a few more times before we leave for Cork."

"Oh, what will we see? Some of the older books? I am so excited. I just wish Papa was here."

Her husband gave her a stern look and said, "Oh, no, you don't. This is *our* honeymoon."

Elizabeth giggled. "Now, Mr. Darcy, you know what I mean. At least when we get back, we will have tales to tell of what we saw to share with my father. He is such a bibliophile, though, he will envy our trip and wish he had traveled with us."

His wife laughed aloud as William muttered under his breath, "Over my dead body." Then they were both laughing.

Fitzwilliam Darcy had a world of respect for the knowledge his father-in-law, Thomas Bennet, had garnered through the years. He even enjoyed some of the first edition copies that the man had acquired that several generations of Darcys at Pemberley had failed to add to the estate's immense library. However, he was delighted that none of his or Elizabeth's family traveled with them on this occasion despite the custom.

***

Once inside the building, they were greeted by the main librarian, who was seated at a desk near the entrance. Immediately coming to his feet, the man bowed to the couple

"Mr. Darcy, how good it is to see you. It has been a while since you visited us last."

"Yes, it has been, Mr. Ryan. Good to see you again, sir." Turning to Elizabeth, he said, "Mrs. Darcy, this is Mr. Michael Ryan, Mr. Ryan, this is my wife, Mrs. Elizabeth Darcy. He and I met nearly three years ago when I traveled here and heard of the priceless antique books the library had acquired."

"It is a pleasure to make your acquaintance, Mrs. Darcy. The staff and I think very highly of your husband."

"Thank you, I am pleased to hear it of him as I think very highly of him as well."

Darcy could feel his face warm with the praise from two individuals who respect he appreciated. As usual, with his shyness, he directed the conversation elsewhere.

"Have there been many new acquisitions since I last visited?"

"Yes, there have been quite a few since I sent you the list of the last group of volumes we had acquired. And I am pleased you have gained a wife. I believe you were still unwed when I saw you last." Elizabeth noted that Mr. Ryan seemed to be suppressing a smile concerning Darcy's marriage status.

"Well, yes, I was." Darcy pulled a little at his cravat then commented further. "We just recently married."

"Just a week ago, in fact." Elizabeth could not resist chiming in, and when she did, Darcy's smile came to the fore letting Ryan know that he was a happy man."

"I am pleased for you, Mr. Darcy, and wish you and Mrs. Darcy the best."

"Thank you, Ryan." Pausing, Darcy hesitated to ask a favor but did anyway. "Would it be possible for us to see the Kells? I know it is not on exhibit, but my wife would love to see it."

"I would? What is the Kells, William?"

"Ah, Mrs. Darcy, the Book of Kells is a marvelous book. Handwritten and hand painted on vellum, it is one of the most beautiful copies of the gospels of the Bible you will ever see. I would be delighted to show it to you since your husband is one of our patrons. He has been very generous in supporting new acquisitions for the library."

"Really now, Mr. Ryan. Mr. Darcy, is it as beautiful as he says?"

"Even more so, Mrs. Darcy. If you will follow me, I will take you both to where the Book is stored. Perhaps one day it will be on exhibit, however, we are unable to safely do so at this time. People are too tempted to touch the pages, and that cannot be allowed as this is an ancient book that needs to be preserved."

Darcy had smiled at his wife despite Ryan answering her question. He knew how excited the man got about one of a kind acquisitions, and the Book of Kells was one that could never be replaced.

As they walked down the long room of the library that cut across aisles with shelves of books, they could see that the library was rather full.

"Ryan, are you running out of room for more books?"

"Yes, we are becoming rather crowded. In fact, the board of directors has even spoken about raising the roof to make it two stories high, however, nothing has been done yet. I think I will believe it when it actually occurs. Dublin's bureaucrats tend to stifle progress, and therein the problem lies."

"But surely Dublin's officials recognize the need to continually support the college's library. After all, knowledge is the key to making progress in our world. Too many things are working to people's detriment instead of their welfare. Of course, the problems with Napoleon have not helped either."

Ryan's mouth dropped open at Elizabeth's comment, and for a moment, he was speechless and turned to Darcy only to find his patron raising both hands indicating he wouldn't interfere. It was only after Ryan understood that Elizabeth was extremely well read from the Greek classics in Latin to Shakespeare as well as some of the novels of the day that he warmed up to this bluestocking that he was coming to like very well. However, he refrained from calling her by that description. He felt Mr. Darcy would not welcome the comment. His instincts were one hundred percent accurate.

"Please tell us more about the Book of…you called it Kells?"

"Yes, Mrs. Darcy. It contains the four gospels: Matthew, Mark, Luke, and John. And it is named after the Abbey of Kells where it resided for centuries. It is believed to have been created around 800 AD. Give me a moment please to uncover the book, and I will give you more information concerning it." After donning a pair of white gloves, Ryan very carefully removed the *Book of Kells* from the protective cloth.

For the next little while, Elizabeth was captivated by the magnificent book that was hand-done by monks centuries earlier. Not only was it beautifully illustrated, it had a history behind it as well.

"The colors are marvelous and so vivid. How can they still look new after so long a time?"

"Ah, Mrs. Darcy. That is why the book is wrapped to protect all the writing and the beautiful illustrations from light and moisture. Great care has gone into protecting this portion of the Bible. It has not only survived Viking hordes but theft of the bejeweled covers and the loss of a small number of pages as well. The text is in Latin and is largely drawn from the Vulgate with a small portion from earlier versions of the Bible."

Darcy sat back and listened to the interchange between Elizabeth and Ryan. He was familiar with the history of *The Book of Kells* and enjoyed hearing his wife's intelligent questions about the book and Ryan's reaction to a knowledgeable woman. For three hours he mostly listened to the two exchange views while interjecting a thought of his own occasionally.

At the end of that time, Ryan sat back and stunned the Darcys with an admission. "Darcy, Mrs. Darcy, for most of my life I have avoided parson's mousetrap as all the ladies I knew had one goal in mind, and that was to marry well. Their interests were mainly feminine fripperies, painting, and music with few other interests. None were compatible with my interests: books. If I could find such a woman as your wife, I would marry her in the blink of an eye, Darcy. I do not know when I have enjoyed a conversation more. *The Book of Kells* is considered one of Ireland's national treasures, but I believe that you have found a treasure also."

Both men smiled as Elizabeth blushed bright pink at the compliment and demurely said "Thank you," which was in direct contrast with the enthusiastic conversation she had just had with the librarian. She gave a small sigh of relief that her mother wasn't there. She would have been chastised thoroughly for acting like a hoyden or a bluestocking for not keeping her questions to herself. As it was, Darcy could not have been more proud of her. He loved Elizabeth for her intelligence and that he could converse with her about books, family, world affairs or the conflicts with Napoleon. And he would continue to encourage her to learn more about any topic she was interested in.

For another hour after Ryan had repacked the book, they looked at some of the older ancient books that were housed in Trinity College Library. And it wasn't long before the Darcys realized that there wasn't enough time during the stay in Dublin to see all they would have liked. So, they made plans to come again the next day.

After bidding the librarian a good day, Darcy and Elizabeth boarded their carriage and headed back to the hotel for luncheon and a brief rest before they would go visit Patrick O'Malley and see which evening would be the best for them to visit his pub. Both were looking forward to the Irish music and dancing that would be featured.

Chapter VIII

After their meal, the Darcys went shopping, much to his wife's pleasure. However, their objective was to purchase a cloak and a bonnet more in keeping with Elizabeth Bennet than Elizabeth Darcy. William himself also had to find a topcoat and hat that would have been more fitting for Mr. Bennet than the master of Pemberley. O'Malley's Pub was not in the worst part of Dublin, but it was in an area where the residents would have resented a nabob and his spouse in environs they considered their own.

The driver of the hack they hired was helpful in knowing where there were a couple of shops that specialized in good used clothing. One had men's clothing of all sorts whereas the other catered to just women's dresses, coats, and accessories of every kind.

"William, I had no idea shops like these were available. In Meryton, older but usable clothing is saved for the poor or for those who have lost their belongings either by theft or fire. We don't sell clothing needed by someone."

"You will find shops of this kind in all major cities, including London. Persons in dire straits will sell what they can sometimes just to be able to eat. In the case of the higher ranked individuals, debts from gambling or poor investments will lead some to these shops in order to fund more gaming. When I first met Patrick, I had to purchase clothing appropriate for going to his pub. A farmer's clothing was all that was available for my size, and it had to be washed thoroughly so I didn't smell like a barnyard."

Both laughed at the thought of a fastidious Fitzwilliam Darcy outfitted as an Irish farmer.

After a couple of hours and the necessity of finding another shop with ladies' clothing, they finally acquired a worn but usable heavy cloak for Elizabeth. A bonnet and gloves had been available at the first shop, but it had been crucial that they find a cloak that would be suitable for Elizabeth as the weather was gradually getting colder as November progressed. By the time they returned to Liverpool, Elizabeth's warmer garments would be needed. But for the moment, this cloak would suffice.

Darcy and Elizabeth had the hack driver take them back to their hotel, so they could change into their purchased clothing and leave their finer coats in their suite. They also decided to take tea before traveling to O'Malley's. Darcy wrote a note to Patrick to inform him they were in Dublin and would see him within two hours and had the desk clerk dispatch it for him.

When they came down the stairs dressed in their used clothing, the desk clerk's jaw dropped. It was all the couple could do to refrain from laughing at his expression until they arrived outside the hotel. Darcy was pleased to note that the hack driver was waiting for them as Darcy had requested. When he gave their destination to the driver, the driver said, 'Yes, sir," and nodded in understanding as to the outrageous clothing they had donned rather than their more expensive garments from earlier. And he thought to himself *He's a smart gent as well as a good tipper.* He would do his best to be their driver for at least part of their stay in Dublin.

***

Arriving at O'Malley's, Darcy told the bartender that Mr. and Mrs. Darcy wished to see Mr. O'Malley and were promptly directed to Patrick's office behind the kitchen.

"Darcy, are ye well?" Patrick O'Malley was nearly as tall as Darcy but was a mite heavier as he stayed well-muscled for keeping the patrons of his establishment in line. It wasn't often that he needed to make his restrictions known to his customers, but for the rare times he did, Patrick made sure he was up to the job as it could entail physically ejecting one or more who had gotten unruly. So, the owner of O'Malley's made sure he was prepared by lifting logs each day to keep his muscles strong. And there were few of his patrons that would challenge him knowing they would be bruised and perhaps even a little bloody if they crossed him. For the most part, his place was one of fun and enjoyment for all.

Darcy winced as his friend grabbed him in a manly hug and lifted him off his feet. When he caught his breath, he said, "I am well, Patrick…and so is Mrs. Darcy."

O'Malley dropped Darcy to his feet and winked at Elizabeth. "And I be seeing the fair lassie that's with ye. Ye are married now? And I be remembering that ye were running from the fair ladies the last time I saw you…what was it? Nigh on eighteen months ago?"

"Yes, I believe so," Darcy said with a sigh. "Now, may I introduce my wife?"

Patrick laughed. "Yes, my friend. I be delighted to meet your fair lady."

"Elizabeth, this is Patrick O'Malley, my good friend and the savior of my life. Mr. O'Malley, this is my wife, Mrs. Elizabeth Darcy."

O'Malley then gave Elizabeth one of the courtliest bows she had ever received as she gave him one of her best curtseys. With a smile, she extended her hand, and Patrick gallantly took it and placed a kiss on her gloved knuckles.

"*Patrick.*" Darcy's scowl caused both Patrick and Elizabeth to erupt in laughter as they found a kindred spirit in each other.

"Mr. O'Malley, as you can gather, I am still training my husband to not be so protective of his wife that he's willing to bloody the nose of a friend."

Patrick roared with laughter while Darcy rolled his eyes and then watched as his friend, possibly former friend, put Elizabeth's hand around his elbow and escort her to one of the chairs in front of his desk.

"Mrs. Darcy, will ye look at your husband now. There he stands with both fists at his side. Ye would think after all the years I've known him that he could take a little bit of teasin' from a good friend."

"Oh, but Mr. O'Malley, you know how high in the instep William is. He still should not take himself so seriously." Elizabeth put her hand aside her mouth and whispered, "After all this time, he still has occasions he wishes not to be teased."

"*Elizabeth!*"

"Please sit, Darcy. Ye know that we're just having a little fun at your expense. What will ye have to drink: port, whiskey, ale, or tea? Mrs. Darcy?"

"A little tea would be delightful. It was a little chilly in the carriage coming here."

"And, Darcy...ere you still speakin' to me?"

With that comment, Darcy gave in and laughed. "Yes, I am still speaking to you, though why I should when you have been flirting with my wife."

Elizabeth immediately feared that her husband had taken umbrage at their teasing but breathed a sigh of relief when it became apparent that Darcy was teasing them.

"Mr. O'Malley, William and I did have our problems at first, but soon I realized that he is the best man I ever met, and I love him dearly. I could not have found a better husband."

"I am pleased to hear it, Mrs. Darcy. He is the best man I know as well. I've always been thankful I rescued the young pup that day from the brigands that would have taken all he had."

"And I am grateful that you did also...else he...." For a moment, Elizabeth couldn't speak.

"But he did, Elizabeth, and I will always be by your side." Taking her hand, he gently kissed her fingers, and his wife blinked away her tears. "Patrick, I'll take a whiskey, if you please."

For a moment, O'Malley paused and looked at the two of them then smiled. "If I found such a woman, I would snatcher up in a moment. You be a lucky man, Darcy."

"Yes, I know."

For the rest of the visit, the Darcys regaled their friend with tales of their trip to Ireland and sighting the dolphins while Patrick told of events that had occurred after Darcy left for home the last time. Just before they left, Darcy told him they wanted to come one evening for the music and the dancing and wanted to know which evening might be best.

"Tuesday be your best. The weekend is when it is verra crowded, and they get most raucous. There will nay be as many on Tuesday. It should be just about right for ye and Mrs. Darcy. A fine evening should be had, and we will delight to show your lady our fine dancers and singers. Will ye be taking a meal as well?"

"Elizabeth, shall we eat here also?"

"You did say the food was good and the ale the best, did you not?"

"We will eat here, Patrick. What will be on the menu?"

"Two specialties of the house: Irish potato soup and Colcannon with bacon and the drinks of yer choice at no charge for my friends."

"We thank you, Patrick, and look forward to the evening. I know my wife will love the new experience."

"And I'll make sure the patrons behave…includin' ye."

All three laughed then they bid him adieu until Tuesday. And Patrick wondered what the conversation would be going back to the hotel. He would love to be a fly.

***

Darcy gave the hackney driver a quizzical eye as he had not asked him to wait for them. "Sir, have you been waiting all this while?"

"Nay. I had some other customers, and since I was still in the area, I thought to check back with you and the missus to see if I was needed to take you back to the hotel."

"Elizabeth, do you have more shopping, or would you like to return?"

"It's been an exciting day, but I am a little tired. Having some dinner and reading for a while would be nice."

"Please take us back to the hotel."

"My pleasure, sir."

Darcy helped Elizabeth into the hackney and settled her on the seat. Both appreciated that the driver kept his carriage neat and clean which was not the case of many of the hired ones. They were impressed with him and his vehicle, but most of all they were impressed with him being available whenever they needed him.

"Hmm. Seems we have a driver that might be useful during our time here. I'm thinking about hiring him for the rest of the fortnight."

"Do you think we would need him every day? We are within walking distance of some of the sights, though it would be nice for most of those days."

"I agree. I believe I will make him an offer that will have him at our beck and call and yet would leave him time for other customers when we have finished with our sightseeing for the day. Perhaps we could make definite plans for some days so that he would be able to accommodate our schedule."

When they arrived at the hotel, Darcy proceeded to see if the man would carry them around town for the next few days. Needless to say, the driver was delighted to have a definite patronage for a period of time without having to hunt for customers. So, a bargain was struck, and the driver would meet them each morning at nine of the clock and be responsible for the Darcys' transportation until tea time. Both men were pleased with the arrangement.

For the remainder of the evening, Darcy and Elizabeth chose to have their dinner brought to their suite and afterwards, they read and then debated the benefits of reading novels such as those written by Mrs. Radcliffe. And, of course, Elizabeth took the opposing position as Darcy suspected she would. This led to quite a discussion that ended when Darcy took his wife in his arms and gave her a kiss that left her breathless. But she still had a question.

"William, were you really jealous when we were visiting with Patrick?"

Her husband just growled, and Elizabeth giggled.

"You know you will never have any reason to be jealous of anyone else. You are the only man for me."

"It does not matter, Elizabeth. You are mine, and there are times when other men look at you and I wish my fist in their face."

"Must you be so protective of me.?"

"Yes, I believe I have been this way since I really looked at you after the coach accident occurred. You were constantly on my mind after that. I wanted to build a fence around you and protect you from all harm."

"Oh, William. I love you so much." And no other words were needed.

Chapter IX

Clouds laden with moisture had moved in during the night, and it was raining cats and dogs when the Darcys awoke the next morning. However, this proved to not be a problem as both were willing to spend the day reading, playing chess, or indulging in more pleasurable activities.

"I see that Mr. Bennet spent quite a bit of time teaching the strategy of chess."

Elizabeth giggled and admitted that she had been playing since she was five years old. On the one hand, she was pleased that she had won the first two games, but on the other she was not sure that she should have. Her husband, being a proud male with a bit of an ego, was not happy that he had lost for he always played to win.

A thought struck his wife, and she stopped smiling and wondered if he was miffed at losing to a woman. "William, is losing the match to me a problem?"

Darcy felt his face grow warm as losing to a female was not the impression he wanted to leave. "My apologies, my dear. Would you believe that I lost quite consistently to my mother when I was growing up when she and I played backgammon?"

"You did? And your mother, was she a good backgammon player?"

"One might say that. If she were still alive, male, and the head of the British army, she probably would have already defeated Napoleon permanently several years ago. She was a very good adversary. Ask Richard the next time he visits. He rarely won a game against her. I was a bit better opponent for her but not by much. All three of us hated to lose, but my sweet mother was the best of us game players. Actually, I must say the four of us because she roundly beat my father on a regular basis."

Both laughed as they pictured his father losing to his wife again.

"But my father loved her dearly. I could not have had more loving parents."

"Tell me about them, please. I've seen their portraits at Pemberley, and I love the one of your entire family when Georgiana was a baby. She was a beautiful child."

"Yes, she was, and she is growing into a lovely young lady as well. And before too long, she will be leaving us for a husband and a home of her own. I will miss her dearly then as she and I have been very close and even more so since my father died." Darcy could feel the beginning of tears pricking the back of his eyes and blinked rapidly to dispel them while Elizabeth pretended not to notice. "Where shall I start?"

"Why do you not start at the beginning? How did your parents meet?"

"Ah, the former Lord and Lady Matlock, Uncle Percy's parents, made arrangements to hold a ball and my father was sent an invitation. My father and Uncle Percy both attended Cambridge together and became friends who stayed in touch even after graduation. Hence, when the Fitzwilliams held a ball in celebration, my father attended not knowing that it would change his life."

"Is that when he met your mother?"

"Yes, and it may have been love at first sight. You've seen Georgiana, and she looks very much like my mother and very little like my father except for her eyes. We both inherited his brilliant blue eyes. However, as you see, I gained all my father's dark looks while my sister has the porcelain skin and lovely blonde hair of my mother." Darcy paused in thought for a minute or two with a faint smile on his face, then he continued. "Father told me he was speechless when he met her because she was the most beautiful woman he had ever seen. When they were introduced, he said he almost forgot to say how pleased he was to meet her. All he could do for a moment was raise her hand and kiss her gloved fingers, and when she blushed prettily, Uncle Percy cleared his throat rather loudly, and Father ignored him. He then asked her for the first dance which she had to decline but accepted him for the second. Uncle Percy said he nearly hauled Father off the ballroom floor when he asked his sister for the supper dance also. Two dances in one evening, and my uncle was going to challenge him if he didn't offer for her before the gossips spread the word over half of England."

"Was your uncle furious that your father was attracted to Lady Anne?"

"I do not believe it was the attraction between them that raised my uncle's hackles. His worry was twofold. And how do I know? He and I sat and spoke for hours soon after my father died. I was only twenty-three, and though my father had been teaching me estate management for two years, it was still a daunting prospect to know that I was now the master of a huge property and responsible for several hundred people as well as my being brother and father to my young sister. It was bad when my mother died as she and I were very close, but it was almost devastating when my father passed. Uncle Percy helped me get through a very difficult time."

Elizabeth quickly noted that Darcy was becoming a bit maudlin about his parents, and she wanted to learn more about the happy times of his family. "You said that your uncle's worry was twofold. How so?"

Darcy blinked and shook his head a little as if he were coming out of a deep reverie. Then he smiled, and his wife gave a soft sigh of relief and returned his smile.

"First, he was a little shocked that Father asked for two dances that evening after just meeting Lady Anne. To the other guests, that meant there was great interest between the two and they might be on the verge of an engagement. Since they had just met, that would not happen if Uncle Percy had his way. That also included his parents as he surmised they would not be happy either. My father was quite wealthy, so they knew he was not a fortune hunter seeking her dowry. And he traveled a bit in the first circles, however he was not a peer nor the son of a peer. His station was a bit above landed gentry but not equal to the peerage, and his parents wanted Lady Anne to marry possibly a viscount or even a duke. This would not happen if she married Gerald Darcy."

"I can see that could have caused quite a problem. But what was the second thing that worried your uncle?"

"It was not a thing but a person: Lady Catherine Fitzwilliam, his eldest sister."

"Lady Catherine as in de Bourgh?"

"Yes, and as the eldest, Lady Catherine expected to be the first to wed and would be a major problem if she was not."

"You mean that she was the same back then as she is now?"

"Not quite as demanding as she is now. She was also a bit more courteous and not so rude as you found her. And, of course, not as violent as to strike someone she despised as she did you for marrying me instead of her daughter Anne having that pleasure."

Elizabeth smiled at her husband as she appreciated that it was a great pleasure being married to him. She could not picture herself wed to any other man as her husband was extraordinary in his love and kindness not only to her but the sheer goodness that he showed to other people no matter their station in life. Reaching over to touch his hand, she squeezed it in a show of support to let him know that the incident with his aunt was in the past.

Where Darcy was concerned, though, it was not forgotten. For his aunt to show up at the ball held right before their marriage and strike Elizabeth in the middle of a dance was unpardonable. He had no desire to see his aunt again but was worried for Anne's welfare. Both had agreed they had no desire to marry each other. In fact, Anne was hesitant of marrying anyone because of her ill health. But Lady Catherine was determined to have Darcy and Anne wed so both estates could be combined. His aunt would have become a prominent member of one of the wealthiest families in England. That was totally at cross purposes with Darcy as he wanted to be the happiest landowner on English soil. And, at the moment, he was.

His wife, however, only tolerated his scowling over Lady Catherine for a few minutes before she verbally prodded him for the rest of the love story between Lady Anne Fitzwilliam and Gerald Darcy.

Darcy stirred himself, shook his head, then continued. "After dancing the first dance, the supper dance, and learning more about her at supper, Father was determined to court and win her affection. At the end of the ball, he asked if he could call on her. He told me many years ago that when he asked, she had the most brilliant smile he had ever seen and knew that she felt as he did. It would only be a matter of time before they were wed."

"And did that happen?"

"Lord and Lady Matlock were not pleased, and Lady Catherine was furious and told her sister she was a fool for even thinking about marrying a gentleman instead of a peer."

"How did your mother respond?"

"She told her sister that she would marry whom she pleased and that she would marry for love."

"I imagine Lady Catherine was not happy to hear those words."

"No, she was not. For the next few months, she either ignored Lady Anne or would harangue her about her duty to the family and her obligation to make a great match. Love had nothing to do with it. My mother continued to respond that she would wed only for love and told me later that it put a schism between her and her sister that never really was healed. That is one of the reasons I never believed my aunt when she said it was my mother's dearest wish that I marry Anne. She always told me to marry for love so that I could be happy like she was with my father."

"Was he finally able to get a courtship?"

"For months, when my Father came to Morningside Manor to call on Lady Anne, the butler, following orders, would tell him she was not receiving callers. He was never allowed to even greet her until one day, her parents were gone, and Lady Anne was in the foyer when Father arrived. The Matlock's butler had just left the front door to place the mail in Lord Matlock's study. When she saw who it was, she invited him into one of the parlors and left the door open. She then asked why he had never called so he told her of the many times he had been turned away. She had been frowning until she heard his explanation and was shocked at her parents' actions. But both were relieved that he was able to see her then as they were nearing the time the Fitzwilliams would be leaving for London to attend the season as part of the *ton*. If he had come three days later, she would have been gone."

"And you would not be here now married to me." Elizabeth felt her heart clench a little at the thought.

"No, I probably would not be." And the thought was devastating to Darcy, and he pulled her onto his lap before continuing the story. With his eyes closed, he held her close until his rapidly beating heart slowed down. Then he gently kissed her and said, "There is more to relate."

"I know, but for the moment, I need a little comfort before you tell me more." She then picked up his hand and held it against her cheek before placing a kiss on his bare knuckles. Both shivered at her actions.

"Uh, should I continue?"

His wife quickly looked up at him. "Of course. I want to hear how they came to be married in spite of opposition."

"It is rather shocking."

Elizabeth's jaw dropped until she thought her husband was teasing her. Then she playfully punched him on his arm. "It couldn't be that shocking."

"Oh, yes it can."

"Do not tell me they were compromised." Elizabeth looked at him with her eyes as big as saucers.

"Let me tell the rest of the visit then you can decide for yourself."

"Very well. I am waiting with bated breath."

"My mother rang for refreshments and continued to quiz my father about his visits. He explained that he was always told she was not accepting calls. Even when he asked if she was ill, he was never given any information. The more my mother heard, the angrier she got at her parents' deceitfulness, for she had been told that my father never called when she inquired. That's when my father told her he had thought about the future that each had discussed at supper the night of the ball. Both had realized how much they had in common and how similar their dreams for marriage and family were. He told her that she had been in his thoughts since that night and apologized for not finding a way to at least let her know he had tried to call on her. He was so caught up with her that he took both her hands and pulled her to him. Apparently, that was too much for both of them because he kissed her passionately, and she kissed him right back. That's when her parents, Uncle Percy, and Lady Catherine walked into the parlor."

"No!"

"Yes, they did. Her parents were shocked speechless, and Lady Catherine shrieked that her sister had been compromised. My father quickly surmised that every servant in the manor would be acquainted with the scene within minutes, and he went down on one knee. 'My beautiful Lady Anne. I cannot live without you and will love you until my dying day. Will you make me the happiest of men by accepting my hand in marriage,' and sotto voce he added 'as soon as possible?' Uncle Percy was the only one who heard the last part. But all heard her joyous 'yes,' and as she threw herself in my father's arms, her father shut the parlor door in the maid's face nearly putting the tea and refreshments on the hall floor in the process. And they lived happily ever after."

At this point, neither one could keep a straight face, and both burst out in laughter.

Finally, Elizabeth caught her breath, giggled some more, and wiped the tears out of her eyes. "I guess it really is not funny, but then again it is." This brought on another round of laughter, and after a few minutes, both sobered up, and she asked, "What happened after that?"

"I was born nine months after their wedding night," William said with a smirk.

Chapter X

Elizabeth and William didn't delay getting to bed as they wished to go to church the next day. He had attended a Catholic church with his father when they traveled to Dublin in 1800; however, things had changed in 1801 when Ireland was incorporated into the new United Kingdom of Great Britain and Ireland. At that time, the Church of Ireland united with the Church of England and formed the United Church of England and Ireland. Other changes were made within the government as well.

William had found the Catholic church ceremony interesting but felt that Elizabeth might be a little uncomfortable. Although he was used to making arrangements without consulting anyone else, he had quickly learned that his wife liked to be enlightened before being told they were going to be doing something whether that meant dining with friends or going to a particular church. So, William consulted with his wife.

"Elizabeth, we have a choice of churches to attend on the morrow. There is a Catholic church in the new part of town and is within walking distance or the United Church of England and Ireland which is further into old Dublin. Which would you like to attend?"

Elizabeth smiled at her husband's thoughtfulness, but she knew immediately where she would like to go. "We are seeing so many new things and learning more about Ireland than I ever thought was possible. But…it would be nice to see something familiar. Could we go to the Church of England and Ireland?"

"Whatever you wish, my love. For my family, it has always been a day of rest and thankfulness for the blessings we have. Our God is a loving god, and my parents instilled that thinking in Georgiana and me. When I was young, Wickham would try to embarrass me because I included the Bible among the other books I read and also because I tried never to miss a Sunday at the Kympton church, even after my parents died. I felt closer to them when I followed through with the good habits they taught me."

"And you learned your lessons well as you are one of the finest men I know."

He was so pleased with her comment, he rewarded her with a kiss.

"What time is the service?"

"In about an hour. Our driver should arrive in about a half hour. We do need to get dressed rather quickly so we can be on time. And we should bring an umbrella as it appears to be raining again. It seems that England and Ireland being united also includes the rain as well."

***

The Darcys did make it to the church on time…just barely. They arrived a few minutes before the music began for the song, and Elizabeth felt a sense of peace as they sang a familiar hymn she knew by heart. Her husband experienced the same and raised his voice in song with a baritone that his wife loved hearing. And after kneeling for the prayer, they listened to a short sermon by the priest concerning Jesus and the Sermon on the Mount.

Afterwards, they were glad they came. The priest, Mr. Godwin, welcomed them and said he hoped to see them again, Darcy mentioned that they would still be in Dublin through the following Thursday week and said they would be pleased to attend. He was delighted that Elizabeth agreed with him.

Mr. Walsh, their hack driver was waiting for them as they exited the church. It was just as well he was close to the entrance as the sky opened up again, and the Darcys got a little wet in spite of their large umbrella.

"Do you mind that we will have another day to spend at the hotel, my love?"

"No, I don't mind. It will give me time to trounce you at chess and backgammon as well and additional time to prove that Shakespeare did not write his plays."

"Really now, my dear. Do you mean to say that someone else wrote Shakespeare's plays?"

"One would get that impression."

"I see. I look forward to our debate. In the meantime, how did you enjoy the service?"

"I enjoyed it very well. I love the songs we sang and the passage of the Bible about the Sermon on the Mount. I've always found that a fascinating study. And Mr. Godwin was brief and an enjoyable speaker. Rather unlike Longbourn's parson, Mr. Edgemont, who can get a bit longwinded at times. Much like Mr. Collins." Elizabeth gave a small shiver of revulsion upon thinking of her father's cousin.

"Don't even mention Mr. Collins. He was so insulting to you with his comments in connection with you and me and our courtship, if I ever see the man again, I will be hard pressed not to give him a facer."

He scowled when his wife chuckled. "I am serious, Elizabeth. The man is a menace. He doesn't know how to speak with a genteel woman like yourself. And I will not stand for it."

Elizabeth took his arm with both her hands and snuggled into her husband's side. "My knight in shining armor. I love you."

"And I love you too."

***

Arriving at the hotel, Darcy released Walsh for the rest of the day after setting a time for him to pick them up on the morrow. They would be going back to Trinity College Library as Mr. Ryan planned to show them a few more of the antique books that were national treasures.

For the rest of Sunday, they would have luncheon then spend a lazy day in their suite. Since their time was their own and they were beholden to no one on this trip, spending a day without interruptions was a luxury they would enjoy while they could.

"Would you like to eat in the dining room today, sweetheart?"

"That would be lovely, William. And am I correct in remembering that they have piano music for us to enjoy as we dine?"

"Yes, that is one of the little refinements that this hotel has. It, including the marvelous accommodations and service are a few of the reasons I enjoy staying here. I hope you are satisfied as well."

"Oh, I am very satisfied with the hotel." However, the gleam in his wife's eye caused him to consider that she may not have been talking about the service.

Nonetheless, they would take time to enjoy the pleasant music and the delicious food before hibernating the rest of the day in their suite. And Darcy sighed as he thought of all the pleasant activities the afternoon would bring.

***

Later, when they arrived at their suite, after a delicious meal of wine, pigeon pie, soup, and a pudding for dessert, Elizabeth found she could not keep her eyes open.

"Are you well, Elizabeth?"

"Yes, my darling, I am well but just a little full and sleepy. I believe I ate too much…but it was so delicious. And I had a second glass of wine, which I never do, and I believe that is contributing to my sleepiness." The small smile on his wife's face caused him to smile as well as he gently put his arms around her, kissed her forehead, her cheek, her nose, and, lastly, her soft lips. She responded to his kiss as she always did, however, her eyes remained closed when he released her.

"Elizabeth," he whispered. "Are you asleep, my love?"

"Mmmm, what, William?"

"I asked if you were asleep," he said against her lips. Elizabeth just smiled and still didn't open her eyes.

So, Darcy picked her up and carried her into their bedroom then began undressing her. He chuckled when he realized he was doing everything, and his wife was half asleep and not lifting a finger to help him. Stripping her down to her chemise, he proceeded to pull the blankets back, lay his wife down, and to cover her with them for warmth. She was asleep before she hit the bed. For a few minutes, he just watched her sleep, taking great pleasure in the beautiful lady he had managed to convince to marry him. Her long, thick lashes brushed her cheeks, and he desired to kiss her senseless but was mindful that she seemed to need the rest. *Perhaps, she is enceinte already. Father said my mother took a nap most afternoons right after they married, and he suspected she might be with child and wasn't surprised when I was born nine months later almost to the day.*

Darcy stripped his clothes off as well and climbed under the covers and wrapped himself around his wife. If he had to wait to make love to her, he would make it as pleasant as he could before she would awake. And as his eyelids drooped, and he laid his head on Elizabeth's shoulder, he smiled.

Chapter XI

The next morning was glorious. The sun was shining. The weather was dry with no hint of rain, and the Darcys looked forward to a leisurely day of sightseeing.

Walsh met them at nine of the clock and took them directly to the Trinity College Library. Mr. Bennet may have been a bibliophile, but his daughter and her husband were right behind him in their love of books, especially ancient tomes.

Ryan met them with a smile and proceeded to give them a little bit more history of the artifacts found in the library. When he showed them the ancient Gaelic harp that had been donated to Trinity College in 1782, Elizabeth gave a sigh of pleasure at being able to see such a thing of beauty.

"Yes, it is beautiful, Mrs. Darcy. It was rumored to have once been in the possession of the last High King of Ireland, Brian Boru, who lived from 941 until 1014 A.D. However, the construction would indicate it was made late fourteenth or early fifteenth century. As you can see, it has nearly thirty strings entailing great skill and much practice to play it properly. And it was associated with the Gaelic ruling class as well. It is very likely that this particular harp was made for a prominent family as you can see it is skillfully constructed and intricately ornamented."

"Oh, to be able to play such an instrument. I do play the pianoforte a little, but very ill."

"My dear, was it not someone of my acquaintance who suggested that practice is necessary for one to become skilled? Ouch!" Darcy jumped as his wife gave his arm a little pinch when he reminded her of her comments concerning his handling of the social graces.

Elizabeth just smiled at him as Ryan frowned a little and wondered what he had just missed. *Ah, well. Perhaps it is just something that is peculiar to husbands and wives.*

Darcy's chuckle alerted Elizabeth to the fact that he was not upset over her reaction though he should have expected it when he was giving her a small verbal pinch. He was a bit relieved that she continued to glean information about the harp.

"Mr. Ryan, what about the provenance of this ancient instrument?"

"Ah, therein lies the difficulty, Mrs. Darcy. Even though the harp bears the coat of arms of the O'Neill's, we have nothing but theories as to the ownership over the next two to three centuries until we reach the last two owners. The very last one was William Conyngham, who donated it to the college. Even so, it is believed to be the oldest harp in existence in the world. And Trinity College Library is privileged to have it among our antiquities."

"I agree, and it is lovely."

Darcy nodded in agreement but wondered what else Ryan would bring them today. He was not surprised when his friend showed them the *Book of Durrow* with which they spent not a little bit of time. This was also a book of the gospels hand written and hand painted and given to the library together with the *Book of Kells*. About a century older than the *Book of Kells,* the *Book of Durrow* was a little more complete than the other with additional information. As with the first book, the Darcys were appreciative of the time and the skill given to the beautiful antique.

They stayed until nearly luncheon and were able to have a closer look at some of the marble busts that lined the Long Room before they left for the day.

"One of the oldest that we have is one you both will appreciate. We have one of Jonathan Swift sculpted by Louis-François Roubiliac. Swift was born right here in Dublin. Since you both are such ardent readers, I'm sure you are familiar with his *Gulliver's Travels* and perhaps some of his other writings, eh?"

Both Darcys nodded their heads as that was a favorite of both that they reread from time to time. Darcy was even familiar with some of Swift's others works also.

"Mrs. Darcy, when we return to Pemberley, you should search the library as we have other of Swift's writings including *Tale of a Tub* and some of his poetry you may enjoy."

Elizabeth smiled as she recognized that her husband was teasing her again because of one of her comments to him as they debated at Netherfield concerning poetry as to whether or not it was the food of love. Her answer to him was, "Of a fine, stout, healthy love it may. Everything nourishes what is strong already. But if it be only a slight, thin sort of inclination, I am convinced that one good sonnet will starve it entirely away."

Darcy was most grateful that the poetry they now shared with each other continued to nourish their love because it was a stout, strong love that would never go away no matter the trials they might face. From Shakespeare's sonnets to Robert Burns and the other poets of their day, the Darcys took the words of love to heart. And Elizabeth pinked just a little when her husband put his hand over hers that was wrapped around his elbow.

Ryan was walking behind them and just smiled at the two lovebirds. Clearing his throat, he began telling them of some of the other busts that could be seen in the Long Room.

"In 1743, fourteen of these busts were commissioned from the Flemish sculptor, Peter Scheemakers. His works include great philosophers and writers of the western world and men connected with Trinity College, some that are famous and others not so famous. Most of his life was spent in London, and many of his works were created there as well. And he was quite long-lived as he died at the age of ninety in 1781."

Elizabeth sighed but said nothing as she considered her father, who was in his fifties, and hoped that his health remained good. She had heard of others even in the 1600s and 1700s, who had lived to their nineties and even into their one hundreds, one even reaching the shocking age of one hundred forty, but she had no assurances that Mr. Bennet would live for several more decades before Mr. Collins would inherit Longbourn. One could only hope.

Darcy spoke softly to his wife. "Elizabeth, are you well?"

Elizabeth gave herself a little shake, smiled, and squeezed her husband's arm. "My apologies. I just had an inconsequential thought that has no place in our enjoyment today. Please ignore my thoughtlessness."

"You are sure?"

"Yes, William...I am sure."

And Darcy had to leave it at that but would address it later when they arrived back at their suite. Anything that would make his wife sigh, as if in sorrow, would definitely be considered. Then he turned his attention back to Ryan's comments.

"Mr. Darcy, will you and your wife be visiting the library again before leaving Dublin?"

"Elizabeth?"

"Perhaps we will. I know I have enjoyed seeing some of the library's treasures immensely. However, I daresay we could spend months perusing the many books and learning more about the wonderful acquisitions and still not see but a tiny percentage of the thousands of things that are here."

Ryan laughed ruefully. "I agree wholeheartedly, Mrs. Darcy. I have been here nigh on fifteen years and have still not seen it all. And probably never will as we keep adding more books that we purchase and many more that are donated from time to time. But it is good to have patrons, such as yourselves, who appreciate the importance of keeping this library alive with the old and the new. You be welcome anytime. Just send word, and I will be available to assist you in any way that I am able."

Extending his hand, Darcy thanked him for all the information he shared with them over the two days. "Let me speak with my wife as I believe there might be one more day when we will return. There are some other first editions she might enjoy seeing."

"Yes, thank you so much. I have enjoyed the visit thoroughly."

With that, the Darcys exited the library and were not surprised to find Walsh waiting for them. Darcy suspected that he had paid the man enough that the driver was able to spend a little time relaxing rather than traveling the entire city looking for business. It was rather nice to have a hack to call their own while in Dublin. It did save time as it was very convenient, and he debated about doing the same when they reached Cork. For now, though, he was hungry and felt that Elizabeth would be ready to eat as well. So, they had Walsh carry them to the other large hotel in town to give them a chance to compare the food with where they were staying. He surmised that it might be difficult to beat.

***

After a nice meal, which could almost match that at their own hotel, they were not surprised to see Walsh near the entrance waiting for them to exit.

"Walsh, did you take time to eat something?"

"Yes, sir. I carries me food, and I eats on the run…so to speak." With that, Walsh gave Darcy a grin that displayed two missing teeth, which bothered the man not at all. Darcy just nodded and told him that he and Mrs. Darcy would like to see how far along the construction of St. George's church had gotten. He and his father had traveled to Dublin in 1800, and there was talk of building the church then with construction beginning within a year or so. Estimated time until completion was about seven years total.

"And I'll have ye to St. George's in the blink of an eye."

Darcy helped Elizabeth get settled on the hack's seat, and Walsh proceeded to keep his word by getting them to the construction site within five minutes.

"My, they really are busy. And there is a lot of materials here."

"Perhaps, my dear, I can find who is in charge, and we can get a little more information."

For a few minutes, Darcy watched the men going to and fro and hauling large stones that would be the walls of the church. He also waited to see if he could determine who was the one giving orders, so he wouldn't have to ask anyone. Soon, he was rewarded as he spotted a man who was definitely in charge and directing the workers in what to do.

"Pardon me, sir. My wife and I were wondering if we might get a bit of information concerning the church."

"I can take a few minutes. What kind of information do ye wish?"

"How is the construction coming? Is it on schedule?"

"He he he. Sir, be ye knowing that it is a rare thing when construction is on time. I place it closer to ten years instead of the seven to eight that was formerly estimated. Weather, not getting the stones on time, and so many other things slow things doon. Not surprisin.'"

"Ah, understandable."

"And how big will the church be when it's finished?"

Surprised that Elizabeth had asked a question, the man hesitated about giving an answer without permission from her husband.

"You will find that I have a very intelligent wife. I too am interested how big as I've never heard any dimensions."

"It will be 84 feet in length and 92 feet wide. But the most interestin' measurement is the spire height. It's to be 200 feet high."

"That is quite high for a spire, is it not?"

"Yes, missus, it is." For a moment, the man did not say more but finally smiled. "Yet, there is a tale going round concerning a bell for the spire. It seems that the architect, Mr. Johnston, had a Gothic church tower built in his garden. Now this tower has a bell in it. And I hear tell that he loves ringin' that bell. Seems his neighbors are workin' mighty hard to talk him into donatin' that to the church for the spire."

"Ooooh! So, you are talking about a big bell, not a small one."

"Yes, missus. That bell is more than big enough for that spire."

With that comment, all three were hard pressed to not burst out in guffaws as they could picture just how desperate the neighbors were to get that bell out of the neighborhood, especially since Johnston loved ringing it. They could just picture the glass in the windows shaking when the bell was rung.

"I am surprised no one has stolen it."

"Perhaps, husband, it is too big to just carry off in the night."

Elizabeth's comment was just too much as all three nearly doubled over in laughter as the nearby workers looked at them as if they were candidates for Bedlam. The threesome could see in their minds' eyes several men struggling to *quietly* and stealthily abscond with a huge bell.

Darcy spoke when the laughter finally died away. "Ordinarily, I do not advocate gossip, but since this has given us some amusement today, I will overlook it. And sincerely hope the neighbors are successful in getting him to relinquish his bell."

This started a fresh round of laughter that caused tears in the eyes of all three, and the surrounding workers just shook their heads and went back to work.

"Thank you for the information. The church should be lovely when it is finished. My wife and I will come back one day, and perhaps it will be finished by then." Extending his own, they shook hands and bid each other good day, and the man tipped his hat at Elizabeth.

As they walked toward the hack, Darcy asked, "Should we go back to the hotel and go to bed early? We are going to O'Malley's tomorrow night, and it will be a very late night. The singing and dancing will go on until two or three in the morning."

"Yes, we probably should. I would like to be awake to enjoy all the entertainment."

"And I guarantee you will enjoy it, my love. There is nothing like an evening at O'Malley's Pub."

Chapter XII

Elizabeth arose early, as was her wont, eager to take a walk if the weather permitted. And the little bit of sun that shone through the drapes on their suite's window indicated it could be a delightful day. True to his wont, Darcy awoke moments after his wife. Even in sleep, he was aware of her every movement whether she was asleep or awake. It never failed to amaze him as it seemed they were tethered to one another

"Good morning, William."

"Mmm, good morning, Elizabeth."

Elizabeth sighed as her husband nuzzled her neck and behind her ear. And even though she wished him to continue, her body needed other attention first.

"You know I love you dearly."

"Mmm."

"However, I must tell you that sleeping with you is a little like sleeping too near the fireplace. I am sweating and would like to refresh myself."

"Later, sweetheart."

"Oh, no. I demand five minutes. And while I am gone, you may keep yourself busy by restarting the fire." With a laugh, she evaded his hands and jumped out of the bed only to let out a loud gasp as her feet landed on an ice-cold floor, the carpet notwithstanding.

Darcy reared up in a panic. "Are you well, Elizabeth?"

At her laughter, he breathed a sigh of relief.

"Yes, my darling. I am well except my feet feel like I am walking on a frozen pond. Where are my slippers?"

"I believe they are under the bed."

"Yes, thank you. I think in future, I will wear a pair of your socks to bed. At least, when I arise there will be something between my feet and the floor."

"I do believe you have made a wise decision, my dear."

"Yes, and I will return in a few minutes."

Darcy blinked as his wife hurried into the spare bedroom and behind the screen in the corner.

With a sigh of his own, he arose and began rebuilding the fire and had it going quite well by the time she returned.

"I should have awakened you earlier to start the fire. It will be a bit before the room is warm enough."

"Then I suggest we do what we can to warm each other until the fire is doing its job."

Because Elizabeth was a good wife, she almost always agreed with her husband…almost…occasionally. And when he was kissing her soundly and nuzzling her until she shivered in delight, she always was in agreement with whatever he wished to do. This morning was no different.

***

As they broke their fast, they discussed their plans for the rest of their stay in Dublin.

"Would you like to go see Dublin Castle today? We would also see a bit more of the city if you wish. And I thought we might take a nap before tea and then take the hack to Patrick's around nine o'clock. The music starts fairly early and continues until the dancers appear at midnight."

"Will we be able to see the inside of the castle?"

"Unfortunately, we will not. My friend, who is a member of the Irish Parliament, has traveled to England with his wife. I had to smile when I read his letter that they were going to Yorkshire to visit his wife's family while we were coming to Ireland."

"Ah, so he married an English lady."

"That he did, my love. He made a trip to London during the season and met her at one of the *ton's* most prestigious balls. Love at first sight, and he wouldn't leave England until she went with him as his wife. Her father finally gave in and gave permission for her to marry the daft Irishman who presented himself on their doorstep for two months before obtaining his consent. Her father said he was tired of seeing the man's ugly face but would miss his daughter dearly."

"Was she in love with him also?"

"Oh, yes. Her father said she bedeviled him the entire two months until he consented. Said she would never love or marry another if her father continued to say no. And because he loved his daughter, he finally gave his permission. I saw him before I left London several months ago, and he said she and her husband are doing well. They have two little boys who will coming to see their grandparents for the first time, and grandpa is elated."

"Do they have any other grandchildren in England?"

"Yes, his two brothers-in-law have five children between them, so the grandparents are not left with no little ones to see and love."

Elizabeth didn't say anything. She just sat very still with a little smile on her face.

Gently picking up her hand and kissing her knuckles, William asked, "What happy thoughts are you having, my dear?"

"I was just thinking how wonderful it would be if we had our own little ones to love."

"I agree. But we do need to wait a little while as it would be at least nine months or a little less into the future."

Elizabeth giggled and sat on his lap. This was her most favorite place in the world. She felt loved and safe as she laid her head on his chest with his arms holding her in a tight grip. She didn't care if it wrinkled her dress or not. She loved this man so much, she would go to the ends of the earth with him. And felt he would do the same for her.

She shifted on his lap until she was turned more toward him as he looked questioningly at her. Pulling his head down to hers, she gently kissed him then opened to him when he ran his tongue over her lips. And she reveled in his kiss.

"Dublin Castle was originally built as a defensive fortification for the Norman city of Dublin. The castle evolved into a royal residence and was resided in by the Lord Lieutenant of Ireland or Viceroy of Ireland, who was the representative of the Monarchy. It has also served as a seat for the English and then the British government of Ireland under the Lordship of Ireland from 1171 to 1541. It was the Kingdom of Ireland from 1541 to 1800, and it is now the United Kingdom of Great Britain *and* Ireland."

"It does not look like the castles I have seen paintings of. How is this one different?"

"It was built at the order of King John of England. Largely completed by 1230, it was typical of Norman courtyard design. It had a central square without a keep and was bounded on all sides with tall defensive walls that were protected at each corner with a circular tower. As you can see, the castle is here at what formed one corner of the outer perimeter of the city. The builders were quite ingenuous in using the River Poddle as a means of defense along two of the sides. The city wall abutted the castle's northeast tower, extended all around the city and back around to the castle to join its southwestern tower. Those who wanted to live within the city walls for safety's sake would pay a tax for the privilege. Apparently, from what I have read, there were craftsmen, tradesmen, and people from many walks of life who lived there serving the needs of those in the castle and other citizens of medieval Dublin."

"Was it really a safe place for them to live? There do not seem to be any city walls that I can see."

"For a time, it was a place of safety from enemies. But not from disease. It was a dirty city with no sewers, so trash accumulated, and the rat population grew."

"The Bubonic Plague was a problem then, was it not?"

"Yes, it was. The city was decimated with the 'Black Death' as the crowded conditions allowed the disease to travel through the population rapidly. People from outside were forbidden admittance until it was determined they carried no contagion. As to the walls of the city, although they had been described as 'huge and mighty and of incredible thickness,' over time, they were eventually torn down and little remain of them throughout the city. Most of the medieval buildings were either burned or torn down at some point, and the only remaining corner tower is this one, the Record Tower."

"Even though most of the original is gone, I would have liked to have toured the castle. I have only seen paintings and never the inside of one."

"Ah, that is what I most wanted to show you, however, we are unable to see it without my friend, Michael, escorting us. Much of the original castle was destroyed by fire in the late seventeenth century, and extensive rebuilding has turned it from a fortress into a Georgian palace instead. This tower is almost the only part of the original remaining. But there is a part of the grounds that I can show you, and they are the Dubhlinn Gardens that are adjacent to the castle. Spring and summer would probably be the best times to see them, but perhaps some of the late blooming roses will still be available."

"Yes, you are a loving husband. You know exactly what I like, and that is the outdoors and the beauty of creation. I look forward to seeing them."

For the next two hours, the Darcys walked the city of Dublin near the castle and viewed what little of the walls remained and the gardens which did not disappoint. Although the weather was chilly, no freezing temperatures had killed off the vegetation until the spring, and they were able to enjoy the roses and several other flowers and any plants that tolerated the cold. And by the time they had seen it all, they were ready to have luncheon, take a nap before tea, and then prepare for the evening at Patrick's pub.

Elizabeth found herself getting excited about dressing down and going incognito to enjoy the Irish music and dance. She was a little acquainted with the instruments and looked forward to the entertainment that was promised. So, a nap was in the offing as she was determined to be wide awake and enjoy the entire evening no matter how late it went.

Chapter XIII

When they awoke from their nap, they ordered sandwiches and tarts along with their coffee and tea as it would be another four hours before they ate dinner at the pub.

Both were refreshed from their nap, and Elizabeth discovered she was ravenous after all the walking that morning and having only a light luncheon. But now, she also wanted information.

"Tell me about the pub. What can I expect when we get there?"

William just chuckled and remained silent as he contemplated what to tell her. He knew she would love the atmosphere once she got used to it. However, it was a little unsettling if one was not expecting it, which was what had happened to him the first time he went there. Patrick had not prepared him at all, and he was almost tempted to leave and not stay for the whole evening. But his friend prevailed upon him, and later, Darcy was glad he had remained after all. He found that he thoroughly enjoyed the music which had a life to it that lifted his spirits. And, though he was a bit surprised at some of the women who danced, he came to understand that it was not much different than the actresses at Drury Lane who entertained with performances of Shakespeare's and others' plays. They were not bauds; they were simply dancing to Irish music that had been around for centuries.

"First of all, there will be the musicians. There will likely be ones playing the fiddle, the Irish bagpipes and even the whistles, but I hope that one of the musicians will also have the bodhrán this evening."

"The other instruments sound familiar, but what is a bodhran? Did I pronounce it correctly?"

"If I did then you did. I cannot give it the Irish or Gaelic lilt that Patrick can. We'll get him to share the proper pronunciation when we arrive. The bodhrán is a small drum played with a stick. My understanding is that it is not a typical instrument but was one that was used for warfare, as a noisemaker at festivals, and by mummers. The man who plays it is very good, and he's an old man who is very familiar with Irish ways."

"I really look forward to the evening. Is there anything else I need to know? You had mentioned that people get a little noisy. Just how noisy do they get?"

"Rather noisy? Very noisy?" William blushed at being put on the spot then added, "They get quite noisy, but they are a good-natured crowd. I will be right beside you, so if the noise makes you nervous, simply move a little closer to me."

"Yes, you would like that very much would you not?" And she gave him a little pinch on his arm.

"Ouch. As a matter of fact, I would." He smiled and waggled his eyebrows at her, and she could not help but smile back at him and chuckle.

For the rest of the while until Walsh would meet them at a quarter of nine o'clock that evening, they read for a bit then played two games of chess and one of backgammon. Elizabeth won two games: the backgammon and one of chess. Darcy realized he would have to improve his strategy if he was going to go head to head with his wife and win an occasional game. Unlike most men, he was delighted that she proved to be a worthy opponent.

***

Darcy and Elizabeth dressed in their plainer clothes and laughed at the difference it made in their appearances. Elizabeth found that she had gotten used to the more expensive gowns—that he said she needed—since she married. Becoming Mrs. Darcy meant that she had to dress the part as well. Now she felt she had gone back to Elizabeth Bennet, and it almost felt a bit strange to her. But she also welcomed the challenge of going incognito and being a little camouflaged as they entered the sphere of another class of people. She would not look down on them. She just realized they were different but still members of the human race and should be respected, and her husband was of the same mind, else he would never think to take her to a pub.

"William, would you help me change the style of my hair. This feels a little too fancy for what I'm wearing."

"The maid did an excellent job of fixing your hair. I love it that way especially the curl lying on your neck."

"William! You must stop that, or we will not make it to Patrick's pub."

He sighed and quit nibbling on her ear and agreed the style needed to be simpler.

"Please help me take it down, and would you brush it for me? It is so long that it is a little difficult for me to get it completely tangle free."

"Yes, my dear. I find great pleasure in running my fingers through your beautiful tresses." Then he proceeded to show her.

When he finished, she twisted her rather unruly curls into a simple bun at the back of her neck and was pleased with the results. "Now, I do not look quite like a nabob, do I?"

"No, sweetheart, you do not. You look like the upstairs maid at Pemberley."

"What! Do you mean my disguise is that effective?"

"Well..."

"Never mind. I know you are just teasing me."

"Yes, and you are so lovely to tease."

"But not tonight. Walsh will be here in a few minutes, and we need to finish our attire and meet him on time."

And they commenced doing just that.

***

"We must have gotten here just in time. This is the last free table."

"And we may find ourselves sharing it as well. It surprised me the first time I came that all the tables are shared. Patrick has too many customers to not utilize all the space. Will that be a problem for you?"

Elizabeth shook her head. "No, I am not that high in the instep that I would refuse to share."

"I knew there was a reason I loved you. Of course, that is not the only reason." Leaning close to her ear, he whispered, "I love your fragrance."

"Ah, 'tis lavender, William. When it is in season, Jane and I would make it in Longbourn's stillroom. Each of my sisters has her favorite. Jane has rosewater, Kitty gardenia, Lydia jasmine, and Mary orange blossom. A friend of my family has a small orangery and lets us have enough for Mary's fragrance each year. It is a beautiful fragrance, but we found that the scents changed depending on which sister was wearing it, and it did not work well for me. However, the lavender is perfect."

"I agree." She sighed as William smiled, took her hand, and kissed her bare knuckles as she hissed in surprise. "There will be retribution for that when we get back to our rooms," she said in a low voice.

"I am counting on it."

Elizabeth could not look at him and keep a straight face. So, she glanced the other way and spotted Patrick at the same time he noticed them. After speaking with one of the waitresses, he then came over to their table.

"Darcy, I'm delighted that ye and yer wife are here. It's good to see ye again, Mrs. Darcy." With that, he picked up her hand and kissed her bare knuckles.

"Patrick!"

"Ye see, Mrs. Darcy. I'm willing to bet that at least one of his hands is fisted. If I not be careful, he will bloody me nose 'fore the evenings done. He is so pernickety. Why don't ye run away with me. I'm not pernickety at all."

"Oh, but, Patrick. Not only is he pernickety, I am also very pernickety. That's why he and I get along so well."

"'Tis a tragedy. Ye are such a beautiful lady, and my friend is a lucky man. One who can also take a bit of teasing."

"Not so much, Patrick. I am verra protective of my new wife."

Patrick grinned and slapped Darcy on the shoulder then extended his hand to the man. "Friends?"

"Yes, we are friends though even my cousin Richard has to tone down his teasing on occasion."

"Mrs. Darcy, is he a tellin' me he wants me to refrain from having a little fun at his expense?"

"I do believe he is, Patrick."

"Then I tink…I'll leave him be…for the moment. Now, what be yer pleasure tonight?"

"You said the other day you have two specials on Tuesdays?"

"Yes, the potato soup and colcannon with bacon."

"Neither of us is familiar with those dishes. Why don't you have them bring us both."

"Aye, Darcy, ye are a smart one. I guarantee ye will love both them dishes. They are the two best we serve. And do ye wish ale with your meal?"

"Elizabeth?"

"Yes, ale would be fine."

"Ye will have it in a few minutes. Enjoy."

"Thank you, Patrick."

As they waited for their food, they glanced around the room and were a bit surprised at the variety of individuals that were seen. There seemed to be farmers in abundance, some who looked like shopkeepers, two that looked like women of the night, several that had to be stable hands, and even several couples who may have been in trade as their clothing appeared more expensive than the majority of individuals in attendance. And all wore smiles on their faces. It seemed that Patrick's was a happy place for gathering together.

Suddenly, the Darcys were not alone at their table as three men and a woman made themselves at home. With a heavy accent, one of the men plopped himself on the end of the bench right beside Elizabeth and turning to her with a smile said, "Ye be a right lass. But I surmises ye be here for the first time as I ne'er seen ye before."

Before William could take umbrage and call the man out, Elizabeth touch his hand that was between them and replied, "Yes, we have recently married, and my husband and Patrick are great friends. He told us of the music and the dancers, and we just had to come."

"New wed are ye? My congratulations, and may I kiss the bride?"

William quickly put his arm around his wife. "Perhaps, you would be happier on this other end of the bench." The scowl he gave the man made the point that a kiss would definitely not be allowed.

The man just chuckled and turned to his friends. "Aye, we got an Englishman with no sense o' humor tonight. We hopes he learns to smile." With that, he got up and sat at the other side of William and began introducing his companions after they ordered their ales. "I be Lochlan, and this be me two brothers, Sean and Liam, and our sister, Maeve."

Elizabeth gave William a little pinch, at which he gave a start, then he too introduced himself and Elizabeth. "I am Will, and this is Lizzy."

Elizabeth couldn't help but smile at her husband's manner with an Englishman's stiff upper lip, and she proceeded to win the respect of all at the table. As far as she was concerned, these were people to be shown regard no matter their station in life. And she would treat them accordingly until finding out they may not deserve it. In the meantime, she was determined that she and William would enjoy the whole evening including their dinner companions.

"I am delighted to meet you and your siblings, Lochlan. Patrick has spoken highly of the entertainment and those who attend, and the enjoyment appreciated by all. Will and I have looked forward to this evening and expect it to be one of the best since we arrived in Dublin."

"Aye, missus, and we congratulate on your marriage. But are ye sure ye found the right one?"

"Aye, I have, Lochlan, the best man in the world. He loves me dearly and has proven himself to be my knight in shining armor when needed. I could not have better."

"Missus, did ye need a knight in shinin' armor?"

Elizabeth blushed and almost didn't answer him, and Will tightened his arm around her shoulders. With a small shake of her head at him, she let him know that Lochlan's question didn't cross any lines other than sincere concern. "Yes, I did. The man was a blackguard and did not behave like a gentleman, and Will became my protector."

"Ye did good, Will, if ye defended Lizzy."

At the compliment, William felt his face warm as he had beat Wickham to a bloody pulp and might have killed him if Elizabeth had not stayed his hand.

"I would have defended her with my life, if need be, Sean. I have loved her for quite a while. In fact, it was love at first sight."

This prompted Maeve to ask, "And how did ye meet Lizzy?"

So, between the two of them, the Darcys related how they were on a coach that wrecked, then how they later met again in Meryton, Elizabeth's birthplace and home.

"Ah, 'tis lucky ye be to meet again, Lizzy."

"Yes, I was most fortunate in seeing him again, Maeve. He is the love of my life."

Lochlan could not resist. He stood and raising his ale—that had just been delivered—he informed the entire room he was making a toast. "To the new weds, Will and Lizzy."

And much to the Darcys embarrassment and William's chagrin, the entire room stood and toasted the couple with much clapping and whistles. So much for remaining anonymous for the evening. With a rueful smile, he turned to Elizabeth and mouthed, 'I am sorry.'

"All is well, Will." And though she was tempted to kiss him on the spot, decorum demanded she refrain especially as it might have brought the house down if she had. She would show him later what a fine time she was having at Patrick's pub and that she liked the informality of Lochlan and his siblings.

Their food arrived, and everyone tucked into the delicious fare. This was the time that Elizabeth began gently interrogating their dinner companions. "Maeve, do you and your family live in Dublin or are you here specifically to come to Patrick's?"

"We nought live here. Me parents owns a farm not too far from Dublin. We comes to town every few weeks for supplies, and we visits Patrick's the night before we heads back. His pub is known for its entertainment, and we's learned to come in the midst of the week ne'er on the weekend when it's packed to the ceilin' with people. At least, we gets to sit while we eat and drink."

There were grins all around and a groan from Liam. "There was a time when we's stood for four hours with nary a break. Me back like to a give out afore we left, and I could sit back at the Inn. Was a week afore it felt normal again."

"Well, I am glad we are all sitting this evening. The food is wonderful, and I am enjoying the company as well."

"Ah, another toast to Lizzy as weel." And the siblings did just so as Elizabeth blushed fiery red and even her husband smiled and toasted her. Her hand on his knee let him know she was pleased.

However, all talk came to a close as the musicians started to play a lively tune to which the audience clapped in rhythm with the music and occasional whistles from to time. The pub fairly rocked with the musicians' efforts and the stamping of many feet. The Darcys joined in, and William was pleased that his lovely wife was having the time of her life.

I am glad I know Patrick and that I thought to have Elizabeth come tonight. And I am delighted she fits in anywhere. I found a treasure I will never let go of.

Chapter XIV

Over the next two hours until midnight, the crowd at the pub applauded the musicians and got raucous singing familiar Irish songs. William and Elizabeth didn't know the words but managed to chime in from time to time with the choruses. He had heard his wife's lovely soprano a number of times at Longbourn, and Elizabeth had heard his singing voice before at church but was again delighted with his deep baritone as it blended in with the voices of the crowd. She was pleased that her husband seemed to have set his stern demeanor aside for the evening whether due to the ale he drank or just because the atmosphere seemed to tolerate only good spirits. As William smiled at his wife, she returned the same to him, and Lochlan winked at his siblings as the singing began to raise the rooftop.

Suddenly, the musicians stopped playing and two servants carried a huge whiskey barrel and set it down in front of the bar. With a quick leap, one of the young men, all dressed in black, landed atop the barrel and began slow tapping his shoes on the hard wood. But it was not a dull tap; it was a sharp one, and Elizabeth was curious what caused such a sound.

"He has metal pieces nailed to the bottom of each shoe that cause that sharp sound. And do not be surprised at how fast he can do that tap as well."

She was enthralled as the dancer began increasing the number of taps until it sounded as if he was doing dozens of taps per minute. Then the musicians joined in and the music got faster and faster, and the dancer kept a perfect tapping rhythm with the playing of the music. However, throughout the entire performance, the man never moved his arms or hands. But his feet kept moving faster and faster as the musicians increased the speed of their music, and the crowd stomped and whistled until it seemed the whole building was rocking on its foundations. And it stopped…as suddenly as it began, and there was a split-second pause and the crowd went wild. It seemed that Kevin McGinnis was a favorite son and a crowd pleaser extraordinaire when he immediately began rapidly tapping until he was tapping faster than he had before and ended his performance with a loud tap, and the crowd scattered as he made a flying leap off the barrel that sent it banging into the bar.

Kevin was swung up on the shoulders of two of the men and carried around the pub as members of the crowd of spectators congratulated him on a fine performance. That is, until he came up to Patrick.

"Kevin McGinnis, ye gave a fine one this evenin', however ye need to mind your leap at the end. Seein's how ye battered me bar again, I'll be charging ye a fee in the future for assaulting it."

The two men lowered McGinnis to the floor, and the dancer proceeded to grab Patrick in a manly hug.

"Cousin Patrick, I'm delighted ye enjoyed me dancing this evenin', but now I have a mighty thirst. Might I have one of your fine ales, eh, cousin?"

"There's no accountin' why me aunt and uncle allowed ye to learn the Irish steps…but I'm glad they did. Ye do bring in the customers, and that is worth a couple of ales and a meal, cousin."

As Kevin got his ale, the bar was cleared of all the dishes and wiped down. Then two women who looked to be in their twenties were lifted to the top of the bar.

"William, I didn't know some women would be dancing tonight…and their skirts are…"

"Yes, Lizzy, they are a little shorter out of necessity. Their ankles must be free for the movements of the dance, elsewise they might trip and fall. It is not considered an impropriety to have skirts of this length as they are still modestly attired."

"I guess I sounded a little pompous for a moment."

"Never, my dear. You were just concerned. However, I did mention that things were more casual here at Patrick's, so you would not be too surprised. Are you enjoying the evening?"

"Yes, very much so. It has been a little noisy, but it is a joyful noise by the people here including you and your siblings, Lochlan."

Maeve giggled then added, "Me and me brothers come as often as we can which is not as oft as we please as the farm keeps us aplenty busy. But 'tis good fun and good food, and when we returns to the farm and me parents, we are ready to work hard again."

"Speak for yeself, Maeve."

"Sean O'Leary, iffen ye weren't such a lazy one…."

"Ach, woman's always complainin'."

"I wouldna be complainin' if ye would finish your own work, Sean."

"Maeve's got the right of it, Sean. When we return, I'll see ye carryin' yer share of the load." Lochlan's glare at his brother caused the man to get red faced, but since it appeared that Lochlan was the eldest, Sean nodded in agreement. The Darcys just pretended not to hear the conversation which ended when the music began for the lady dancers and the entire pub stilled which caused Elizabeth's jaw to drop when it got almost dead quiet.

The music began softly, seeming to mainly be the whistles, and gradually picked up in sound as the women danced upon the bar. Elizabeth was intrigued at how different it was from the dancing with a partner like she was used to. Again, there was little arm or hand movement, and the women danced in very small spaces upon the bar. Elizabeth smiled as she could see that some of the movements must be similar to the ballet she had read about that was gaining in popularity throughout Europe. The women were wearing soft slippers that were tied to their calves with ribbons that disappeared under their skirts. At times, they were up on their toes for part of the dance then did a little to-and-fro movement after which they each moved to separate ends of the long bar with a skip or a hop and even a little kick at one point. The dance went on for several minutes with the simplicity and the beauty of it keeping the audience enthralled. Then it ended with each of the women bowing to the audience then doing a deep curtsey as well. The crowd in the pub went wild with cheers, clapping, and whistles, and when the noise finally died down, it was time to go home.

Will and Lizzy said their goodbyes to the O'Learys and let them know how much they enjoyed their company. Their tablemates wished the Darcys long lives and the wind at their back, knowing they might never see them again but grateful for the time they had spent together.

"Patrick, thank you for an enjoyable evening. The food was delicious, and the entertainment was grand. However, the ale could have been a little better."

"Darcy, me boy. You be pullin' me leg. I've the best ale in town and intend to keep it that way."

"It is not often that I get the best of you by teasing, Patrick. The ale was excellent."

"I do believe, Patrick, that I have experienced a side of my husband I have not seen before. And I am delighted to see him lighter of heart and genuinely enjoying himself. William, perhaps we can come again before we leave for Cork?"

"My dear, your wish is my command."

"Yer sweet wife and ye are welcome anytime. 'Twas my pleasure to host ye both this evening. Didn't I tell ye I had well-behaved customers?"

"Yes, you did, and we thoroughly enjoyed the O'Learys who shared the table with us. They simply added more interest to the evening."

"They's good people."

Others began demanding some of Patrick's time, so the Darcys bid him goodnight and headed out the door hoping Walsh would be there on time.

At first, they didn't see him, then Elizabeth said, "Is that not him two shops away?"

"Yes, that is his hack."

But when they started toward the vehicle, two men came out of the shadows and demanded their money. Elizabeth's scream alerted the O'Learys who had not gone far from the pub and in a few moments, the men were on the ground, the result of flying fists. Hearing a commotion outside, Patrick had appeared.

"Darcy, are you and the missus well?"

"Thankfully, yes, due to the O'Learys quick action. Can you make arrangements for the magistrate to take custody of these men?"

"Yes, but I want some answers first."

"As do I, Patrick."

"Why did ye accost these people?"

At first, they wouldn't respond, but when the pub owner jerked one to his feet, the man answered that they figured the Englishman had money. He and his cohort had overheard that the Darcys were on their honeymoon and determined they had to have money to travel so far, and he and his partner were going to relieve them of it.

"Well, this is one Englishman you should have avoided. Instead of money, you may have earned the hangman instead. And if you had harmed my wife, I would have…." Darcy was so angry that he was ready to beat both of them to a bloody pulp.

"William, I am well. Please let us try to end the evening on a happy note. It has been lovely so far."

"Very well, Elizabeth. It is just that…."

"I know, William. But all is well."

Darcy sighed and snugged his wife to his side and tried to end his thoughts of what *could* have happened.

"My friend. Ye and yer wife go and dinna worry about this business. I know the magistrate personally and am willing to testify to what happened. I doubt ye will be needed at all." Turning to the O'Learys, he said, "And for protecting me friends, ye will have free meals and drinks the next time you come."

"Ah, Patrick. 'Tis a good man ye are. 'Twas our pleasure. We like Will and Lizzy and wish them the best." Bidding them goodbye, Lochlan and his siblings turned and went to their lodgings.

"Will and Lizzy?"

"They introduced themselves. We had to do the same but kept it more informal. No last names."

"Ah. Probably 'tis wise." He paused. "Go home. Rest. Tomorrow is another day. And, Elizabeth, I pray ye will not suffer from this incident."

"I am well…I think, Patrick. A little shaken, but only a little. Thank you again for a lovely evening and for seeing to these men. I do need to get home and to rest."

"Sir, are you and the missus well?"

"Yes, Walsh. We just had a little problem with two men who decided to rob us. But all is well."

"Very good, sir. Ye and the missus ready to return?"

"Yes, please. The sooner, the better." Putting his arm around Elizabeth, he guided her to the carriage and helped her in.

Once she was settled, her reaction set in, and his wife began to shake.

"Elizabeth, my love." Taking her on his lap, he cradled her in his arms and comforted her determined that she should sleep late in the morning, and he would not disturb her until she was feeling better.

But Elizabeth needed more comforting, and the evening ended on a happier note.

Chapter XV

Over the next week, the Darcys had Walsh drive them hither and yon as they looked for more of Dublin's offerings. They didn't mind that lack of exact planning in their travels around the town as they gave Walsh instructions to just take them to new places. However, they did request him to carry them to Christ Church Cathedral and St. Patrick's both of which proved a bit discouraging. It was not that the cathedrals were lacking in size or a type of beauty, but they found it disappointing that the two buildings were experiencing a lack of maintenance, which was contributing to major problems that would eventually require major repairs. It was not known if it was a lack of money or just a lack of interest or even the original construction that might have led to problems later on.

St. Patrick's was of special interest because Jonathan Swift had been dean there for thirty-two years. During his tenure, his most famous sermons and his 'Irish Tracts' had been given. Although the Darcys wished to see the cathedral where he served as dean, they found it was closed to visitors due to repairs that were being made. The priest made it clear that certain parts of the building were not safe to traverse, but he allowed them to stand in the entrance and see what they could from that vantage point. It satisfied some of their curiosity about the large building but not all.

A few days before they were to return to Patrick's pub one more time and leave for Cork two days later, they hired a coach and traveled about 30 miles through the Irish countryside. As Ireland was still lacking freezing temperatures, the landscape was still very green in many places proving that the nickname 'Emerald Isle' was very appropriate.

"William, this part of Ireland is beautiful. I've never seen grass so vivid green before. And many of the flowers are still in bloom. I love the cottages with their flower boxes and climbing roses or ivy that covers the walls. They are so charming."

"Yes, they are pretty but not as beautiful as my lovely wife."

Elizabeth smiled at her husband but refused to let him kiss her while the coach was moving as they were periodically hitting ruts that tossed them about in spite of Darcy holding his wife. "I love you, my dear, but I would prefer not to get a split lip." Instead, she kissed her finger and then touched his lips, and he was satisfied…for the moment.

Later, they stopped for the night at a small, but clean inn and planned to leave early the next morning. Travel back to Dublin would take most of the day, and they wished to view the Glendalough monastic settlement near the two rivers confluence which had formed two lakes: an upper lake and a lower one. They would have to view the settlement from a distance, but that would allow them to see some of the wildlife as well as the ruins from the twelfth century.

***

Early to bed and early to rise saw them on their way at the crack of day when the purples, pinks, and yellows were just appearing on the eastern horizon. The four outriders Darcy had hired would stay close to the coach with the driver and a spare riding on top as they had the preceding day. After the incident at Patrick's, he would not take any chances with his wife's safety.

"Oh, William. It looks like we have a beautiful day to travel. Should we have the innkeeper make up a food basket? We might take a walk and see some of the animals of this area. And I do wish to walk."

"Are you getting a little homesick, Elizabeth?"

A little bit. I do miss my daily outing and my walks to Oakham Mount. And, of course, I am missing the paths of Pemberley now as well. Although I'm enjoying our trip, I *am* a bit anxious for home."

"We will be home within little over a fortnight. Do you think you could wait that long? And we still have Patrick's to visit again, our voyage to Cork, and many different sights to see there also." He then gave her smile that melted her heart and made her knees weak. "I want to show you off to my friends at Blarney House as well because I married the most wonderful woman in the world."

"Impertinence and all?"

"Of course, but most of all I want to show you the inside of a castle."

"A castle? Which castle?" A smile broke out on Elizabeth's face, and Darcy wondered if he should take her to more than one castle if it made her that happy.

"Blarney Castle near Cork. My friends live in Blarney House and own the Castle. We can tour the castle and find out something that makes them rather unique from other homes."

"Oh, tell me now. I can't wait."

"No, no. You will have to be patient a bit because this is something I have to show you and explain why it is the way it is."

"Ah, a riddle...for me to solve?"

"Perhaps. And if you solve the riddle, what would you like as your prize?"

"Mmm." Elizabeth thought for a moment. "I would like fifty kisses."

"*Elizabeth.* We would never get past the first one."

His wife cocked her head, furrowed her brow, then said with a smile, "I do believe we would not." And she quickly gave her husband a kiss before the coach hit another rut.

***

Darcy had the two coachmen watch for a place they could stop so they might view one of the lakes and the settlement where the monastery had been set up. The first spot didn't give them much of a view, but the second gave them the ability to see the entire valley. Although the wind had a bit of a chill to it, they found it was warm standing in front of the trees in the direct sun.

"How beautiful it is with the sunshine reflected in the lake. Oh, are those goats on the hill?"

"I believe they are. They must have gotten away from their owners as I do not think that they are mountain goats as they are not indigenous to this area."

"I wish they were," Elizabeth said, with a sigh. I've never seen mountain goats before. Only paintings in some of Papa's books."

"If it will make you feel better, I have not seen them in person either. Their horns do seem rather more formidable than those on farm animals."

"And I gather that they use those horns for dueling?"

Darcy looked taken aback for a moment then chuckled at his wife's comment. "Ah, yes. They will fight over who wins their lady love, and I imagine it can be quite the battle."

Both were silent for a few minutes as they looked over the valley with what was probably the smaller lake within view. Elizabeth breathed a sigh as she felt the peace of the place all around her, and she laughed at several of the robins fighting over some seed heads. Looking down at her, William smiled and felt he could not have chosen better than Elizabeth, and his heart was content.

"Elizabeth, if you look down to the right of the lake, you can see the ruins of the Glendalough settlement. And toward the back of the ruins, do you see the tall tower?"

"Yes, I see it. It looks like a huge lighthouse."

"Have you spotted the few windows it has?"

"I see three. But what was the tower for?"

"Apparently, it was in case of raiders. In the early years, that was a problem with being attacked, and the residents were prepared with the tower. There was a tall ladder at the bottom that was pulled up once everyone was inside. Raiders were unable to ascend to the upper reaches of the tower, and the monks were safe for a period of time."

"Unless the raiders decided to conduct a siege. To withstand that, they would need quite a bit of food and water stored there."

"And that may be why it is so tall. The inhabitants may have been able to outlast a siege if they had enough supplies."

"Perhaps."

"Do you see the waterfall beyond the tower?"

"Yes. I did not expect that. Is that from the upper lake?"

"Very likely, and it may be fed by winter snow with the spring melt."

"Shhh. There's a fox. Is he not beautiful?"

"Yes, he is quite handsome…for a fox."

"Yeees. Oh! Do not tell me you rode to the hounds, William," Elizabeth hissed at him.

"Steady, my love. To my shame, I did but only once."

"What happened?"

"I was close enough to see the hounds start tearing the animal to pieces while very much alive. I rode up to scatter the hounds but before I could, the animal looked up at me and the spark in its eye died. I swore I would never go again."

"What about the other men?"

"Two of them rode up to me and demanded to know 'what the devil I thought I was doing.' I was so angry, I wanted to give both a facer, but it would not have helped the fox. So, I answered, 'Nothing, I've done nothing.' And I turned my horse and went back to the stable and never had anything to do with them again."

"You do not hunt at all?"

"Yes, but only for good reasons. On my various properties, there are herds of deer. On occasion, the herds outgrow the available food in the area, and there is danger of starvation. My men and I will hunt, not for sport but to cull the herds of some of the older animals. In some cases, we will take a small number of younger ones that we share with tenants, especially those who may have been sick or been hurt by the weather damaging or destroying their crops. The venison we bring can make winters much easier for them. This benefits the tenants and keeps the herds strong."

"Fitzwilliam Darcy, you are a good man." With that, she pulled him behind a big tree and kissed him like she hadn't seen him in a year. Needless to say, he returned her kiss with ardor.

"Mr. Darcy, Mr. Darcy." The frantic call came from one of the outriders. "Are you well?"

Darcy chuckled and called back that he and his wife were well and were simply behind a big tree, safe and sound.

"Very well, sir." Both stifled their laughter and wondered if the man was blushing at his mistake.

"And that is a good man also, Elizabeth. His orders were to keep us in sight and make sure we were safe, and he is doing his job. Remind me to give each of the men a bonus when we arrive back in Dublin. All of them have been very attentive today."

"Is it necessary to have them so watchful?"

Darcy frowned then answered her, "I do not want a repeat of what we experienced at Patrick's at the end of the evening. Isolated places like this could be frequented by highwaymen, and I would prefer not to take chances especially since I have precious cargo with me."

Elizabeth gave him a little smile and laid her head on his shoulder. She decided she would be his precious cargo any day he wanted her to be. She was very glad she had accepted when he offered for her. There would never be another man for her.

The Darcys stayed long enough to enjoy the view, see various birdlife, and even spot more goats on the sides of the hills. While they had been enjoying the beautiful scenery, one by one the outriders and the coachmen had eaten the lunch packed by the innkeeper's cook while the others kept an eye on the road and the Darcys. William and Elizabeth had taken a half hour to do the same and then to feed the crumbs to the birds and two squirrels who showed up begging. But they couldn't stay all day. They needed to get back to Dublin before dark. Arriving in darkness was just looking for trouble, and William wouldn't allow that.

Chapter XVI

Elizabeth and William were greeted with open arms when they arrived at the pub.

"Darcy, Elizabeth. 'Tis grand to see ye both again. Will he be stayin' a while longer in Dublin?"

"Only until Thursday. Then we leave for Cork."

"And ye be leavin' on that ship of yor'n?"

"Aye, we will travel on the Clipper ship to Cork, and after staying for about a fortnight, we will return to Liverpool then Pemberley."

"One day ye'll have to take me on that ship that I understands flies like the wind."

"It is certainly much faster than the larger ships. She was made for speed. When next we come, I promise that we will take you sailing one day."

"I look forward to it. I been only on a big ship once heading to Cork. Took us nigh on three days to reach the Port of Cork, and we's had only one stop along the way."

"We should only have to travel two days to get to Cork. I must confess that I am a bit spoiled. When I began managing my estates, I was very impatient to get things done, especially traveling to Scotland and Ireland to meet with my stewards. It seemed a waste of time to spend so many days just to get to the estates. So, when I had the opportunity to buy the clipper ship, I jumped at the chance and have never regretted it. It saves me time and money and is a pleasurable way to travel. In fact, on one of those trips, Captain Lowery allowed me to join the men and help set the sails."

"William, that is hard work." Elizabeth bumped his shoulder and spoke in a loud whisper, "And you became a common sailor for the day?"

"I will have you know, Elizabeth, it takes great skill to handle the ropes on a clipper that is nearly double the speed of a much larger ship," he said with a smile.

"Aye, but you have the muscles with which to do it," said she.

"But not the skill at first. I nearly got swept overboard that time when the boom swung around, and I barely missed it sweeping me across the deck."

"Oh, William. I am delighted it missed you rather than me missing you." Elizabeth took his arm and leaned into his side as he patted her hand. But he noted that she shivered just a little.

"Are you cold, Elizabeth?"

She shook her head. "No, just a thought of when we were here last."

"Patrick, could you have one of your big, burly servants escort us to our carriage tonight when we leave. I believe my wife would be more comfortable if there were no repeats of the other night."

"Be me pleasure, Darcy. And I knows the man: O'Shannassy. He ere twice as big and twice as tough as any man I ever seen. And he boxes bare knuckled. No one who comes here crosses him. He's the best man I got."

"Very good. Thank you, Patrick."

"There are not as many people tonight. Is the weather the problem?"

"Aye, Elizabeth. The rain and the wet diminishes a crowd but only durin' the week. On a Friday or Saturday they will come even if the snow is three feet deep. On some winter days, I have them slidin' in the entrance."

All three laughed as they pictured customers gingerly walking across icy ground and sliding in the front door on their backsides.

"I got ye a table in the front to the side. Ye should have it to yeselves tonight. Will ye have the potato soup and colcannon again or do ye wish to try somethin' new?"

"William?"

"I enjoyed our meal the other night."

"As did I, and we have eaten very fancy since then. I think I would like the soup and colcannon. It was very good. And do you have something sweet for afterwards?"

"Just the t'ing. Me cook has done several apple pies that melt in ye mouth. Guaranteed."

"Oh, it sounds wonderful. I have not had apple pie since September. Thank you."

"Don't be thankin' me nowt as we do this on the nights when the crowd is smaller. When the place is filled, the only t'ing they be wantin' is their meal and ale or Guinness. Cook is too busy with the other food and refuses to bake the sweets. So, you'll have all the apple pie ye wish."

Elizabeth's eyes lit up, and both men laughed at the smile that graced her face as she thought of endless pie. But Darcy also had to admit that apple pie sounded marvelous to him as well.

***

The evening turned out to be a very enjoyable one as the Darcys discussed their trip to Cork and their plans after arriving. They missed the O'Learys but didn't miss the large crowd that had attended the week before. An evening that was a mite quieter was appreciated after their pleasant trip to the country the previous two days. The food was as good or better than the prior week, and Elizabeth and William both ate two big pieces of apple pie. Having a sweet tooth was only one more thing they had in common.

"You are aware that we both need to take a long, brisk walk on the morrow as penance for overindulging in an apple pie that was more than delicious."

"And I do not regret it one whit." Then he smiled and winked at her.

The music was also enjoyable and different from the prior Tuesday as the older man with the bodhrán came and joined the other musicians. It gave a more strident sound to the music, and

Elizabeth could understand why it had been used during wartime and festivals rather than being used as a regular musical instrument.

"How is he changing the sound of the drum? I thought they always had the same tone."

"I do not know. The old man has been playing it for several decades is my understanding and has apparently been involved in more than one conflict in this country. Perhaps that is why he favors the bodhrán."

And the old man raised his head and looked both over as if he was aware they were speaking of him. Elizabeth shivered as though someone had walked over her grave as the old man slowly shook his head, lowered it, and continued with his playing and never looked at them again. Darcy refrained from telling Elizabeth that the man had lost all his family in the fighting of 1760 and the Irish Rebellion in 1798. The English soldiers that put down the rebellion had a record of not extending any mercy to anyone who had been involved. And this lack left many Irish families bereft of loved ones who perished under terrible circumstances.

No, she has no need of that information. It would only make her sad. Instinctively Darcy knew how soft-hearted his wife was concerning animals and people that were helpless or victims of injustice. He didn't need to be told of how her heart broke the day one of the barn cat's kittens perished under the hoof of one of Longbourn's horses that took a misstep. *No, I'll keep that information to myself.* And he hoped she would never find out the man's history.

***

The Darcys were delighted to see that Kevin McGinnis was dancing again this evening. Elizabeth was enthralled that anyone could move their feet so fast. However, this particular night, his performance had more of a military feel to it. Both William and Elizabeth noted the difference but refrained from commenting. Perhaps the inclusion of the bodhrán was what prompted it. No matter, as they would not say a word about it until back at their suite.

Although they enjoyed the music and Kevin's dancing, the atmosphere in the pub was different that it had been the prior Tuesday. Just a bit of tension and not quite as happy as when the O'Leary's were there. And when Kevin finished, they found out why. Patrick walked up to his cousin and asked, "Are ye sure ye wish to do this?"

"Aye. Robbie and I have been practicin', and he be determined to beat me tonight."

"Ye do know that ye will have to have the bar refinished."

"Aye. I already have the money, Patrick. Let the contest begin." And Kevin rubbed his hands together with glee, certain he would beat Robbie.

Patrick raised both hands in the air, and the customers quieted, wondering what was in the offing.

"Ladies and gents, we have a surprise for ye this evening. Mr. Kevin McGinnis and Mr. Robbie O'Hanlon have agreed to have a contest as to who has the fastest feet in Dublin. And, they have agreed to let ye decide who is the best."

At an indignant cough from Kevin, Patrick looked at his cousin as if he was something stuck to his shoe, then he laughed and said, "Pardon me, *Mr. McGinnis,* the one who has the fastest feet in all of *Ireland.*"

That was all it took, and the customers joined in the fun, whistling, and shouting until finally they quieted for the contest.

The keg Kevin had danced upon was removed as well as all the glassware and dishes from the bar. Then the two men sprang to the top of bar and stood eyeing one another with grins. All was quiet while Kevin explained that the customers would be allowed to judge who was the best dancer of the two by their applause and shouts of praise. This brought on a multitude of clapping, whistling, and stamping of feet. Then again, all was quiet as Kevin started out tapping his feet slowly, and then he was gathering speed until it seemed that he was making at least two dozen or more taps per second, and the crowd went wild.

***

Even though the crowd was not as large as the prior week, these customers were just as noisy in their appreciation at the end of Kevin's performance. But, again they quieted as they waited to see how good Robbie was.

"Do you think he will equal Mr. McGinnis' performance, William?"

"I have no idea, my dear. I had not even seen Kevin when Father and I were here in 1801. Patrick had only the musicians. No dancers were here."

"Mr. McGinnis seems pretty sure of himself and his abilities."

"Ah, I see you have also noted he has a bit of ego. I admit that I am curious to see if the other man can beat him at his own game. But we should see the results in a few minutes."

And it turned out that Robbie had an ace up his sleeve. He started out slow and began increasing in speed, then he started slow again and went a little faster than the first time. And he did it again even faster still. And the fourth time he slowed then sped up the pace, it was as if his feet were on fire, and the pub rocked with the noise of the crowd that included the Darcys. Robbie finished and bowed to the crowd as Kevin looked on with a scowl on his face.

"Now ye determines who ere the best in Ireland. Who believes it is Kevin McGinnis?"

And the crowd roared their approval.

"Who t'inks it is Robbie O'Hanlon here?"

And the crowd roared their approval again.

As Patrick raised both hands, the roomful of customers quieted, eager to hear the decision.

"I could nay hear the difference." And a groan went through the room.

"Let's do it again." So, the crowd voted again with hoots and hollers, stamping of feet.

Patrick stood at the front and announced, "I calls it a draw. I canna tell that there is a difference as both have feet of lightning as they must have paid the little people some gold to give them the talent they have." And since Patrick was a brilliant businessman, he said, "And an ale for everyone." The groan of the crowd then became a shout of appreciation, and Kevin and Robbie shook hands and looked forward to a drink after their exertions.

Elizabeth was surprised when William got up, took her hand in his, and they approached the two men.

"My wife and I enjoyed your performances very much. May we stand for meals and ale or Guinness for you both in appreciation?"

"Thank ye, sir. Robbie and I are Guinness men."

"Yes, thank ye. Tonight was a wee bit of fun between Kevin and me. He's been teaching me the footwork."

"Aye, and he turned out to be a better student than his teacher…almost." Kevin grinned and slapped Robbie good naturedly on the back as his student aimed a playful punch to Kevin's arm.

"Ach, these two have been in each other's pockets since they were in leadin' strings, and I doubt that will change even after they are wed next spring."

"Oh, congratulations are in order then. Patrick, see that they get two Guinness each this evening along with their meals."

"But how do you learn to move your feet so fast?"

"Oh, missus, it takes a great while to learn to how begin tapping the shoe. I naye couldna show ye how we start in a few minutes. Takes many an hour and much hard work to learn."

"Are only men doing this type of Irish dance?"

Kevin turned red faced as Robbie poked him in the ribs.

"Missus," Robbie whispered, "Kevin ere teaching his fiancée how to tap, but no one knows." And he almost giggled like a lass.

"*Robbie.* Mind ye words."

Patrick's jaw dropped. "But Corrine could not tap in a skirt." And his eyes widened as he gained understanding of what he was saying. If his cousin's fiancée was dancing in trousers, he wouldn't be one to bandy it about. Not a soul added to his comment.

"Patrick, we are leaving for Cork day after tomorrow. Perhaps we could give our leave tonight."

"Yes, Patrick. We have loved being here. The musicians, the dancing, the food, and even the customers have been wonderful fun. Thank you so much for having us here."

"Elizabeth, ye and Darcy be welcome anytime. Though it be a long while afore we sees ye again, may you have fair winds and God bless ye as ye travel and return home safely. Darcy, my friend, t'ank ye for bringin' ye beautiful wife. It was me pleasure to meet her." With that, he kissed Elizabeth's bare knuckles as Darcy just rolled his eyes. And Kevin and Robbie guffawed at Darcy's expression.

"Ye see, Kevin. I tells ye that himself has his hand fisted at his side ere I'm his friend."

"I sees it. Perhaps it be best ye not tease him quite so much, Patrick."

"William, you must not be so protective of me."

Darcy blushed, and his ears turned pink as he quipped, "But I cannot help it, my dear. I feel every man wishes to run to Gretna Green with you, and you are mine."

Elizabeth smiled at the look in his eye and held his arm closer. The three other men just nodded at one another as they recognized the great love the Darcys had for each other. That was the type of marriage the two younger men desired and were hopeful of achieving in the spring.

As for Patrick, he had yet to find a woman to hold his heart, but he hoped the future would bring one as marvelous as Mrs. Darcy. He was happy for his friend.

"It is time to go, my love."

Elizabeth just nodded with a smile. Saying their goodbyes, they headed to the pub door with O'Shannassy close behind. There would be no robbers about tonight.

Chapter XVII

Two days later after saying their goodbyes to all they had met and spent time with, the Darcys and the crew of Pride of Pemberley headed to Cork. The journey would be twice as long as the one from Liverpool, and they would stay overnight at Waterford Port thus taking two days to finally reach Cork. They were prepared to leave before sunrise and weighed anchor as the golden orb made its appearance.

"Are we making good time, Lowery?"

"Yes, we are doing very well. Since it is remaining clear, if the wind stays with us, we should arrive in ten to eleven hours at most. Weighing anchor at dawn and light traffic allowed us to get a good start to the day. If the weather holds, we should be at Cork by tomorrow night."

"Is Mrs. Darcy well?"

"Yes, she said she is quite well, just sleepy."

Lowery, with a slight smile, raised an eyebrow in an unspoken question.

"We were up a bit later than we intended."

Lowery's eyebrow inched a little higher.

Darcy chuckled. "It's not what you think. She beat me soundly at backgammon, two games in a row, which my manly pride would not let go unchallenged. It took two more games before I finally regained a win."

"Wasn't it backgammon your mother played so well?"

"Mmm." With a sigh, Darcy nodded in agreement. "My mother held her own against me and my father. Very rarely did we win against her. Chess was a little more even as we all seemed to win about the same number of games." He paused. "And I miss them dearly. Not a day goes by that I do not think of them at least once."

"You are a very lucky man, my friend. Wonderful parents, and now you have married a wonderful woman. She is genteel, courteous, appreciative of what is done for her, and she is a lady through and through to boot. She reminds me of my Carly."

"Would you ever consider marrying again if you found another good woman?"

"Nay. Carly was one of a kind. I lost my heart and never got it back. It died when she and my son died. What I have left is for the sea. She is my mistress now, and if I'm lucky, I'll die and be buried at sea."

"I will see to it if I can."

Lowey just smiled and closed his eyes and saw his wife when she was alive and happy in his mind's eye. Then he straightened and asked, "And if anything happened, would ye remarry?"

"No. Elizabeth owns me, heart, mind, body, and soul. If something happened to her, I might die with her. My father died a piece of him at a time over seven years until his heart finally gave out. I would probably follow in his footsteps whether I wanted to or not. Elizabeth is my life."

"And you are sure she is well?"

"Darcy smiled and nodded. "Yes, I am sure. I surmise that we might be adding a child to our family in a matter of months."

Both Lowery's eyebrows went up this time.

Darcy laughed aloud. "Do not be surprised. I was born almost nine months to the day after my parent's wedding night. My mother had more naps, in the afternoons and occasionally mornings, than I had ever seen before when my sister was born. Father said she did the same with me."

"Like father, like son?"

"Perhaps, I am more like my father than I realized. At least, I hope I am as good a husband and father as he."

"I have no doubt. You are a good man, and you married a fine woman. I wish you the best."

"Thank you."

***

Two hours later, Darcy went below to find Elizabeth wide awake.

"Have you been awake long?"

"No, just a few minutes. However, I am hungry. I doubt it is time for luncheon, but the cook did pack some fruit did she not?"

"Yes. Would you like some? I think I could use an apple and some water about now."

While they ate, they chatted about what they would see and do in Cork the next day if weather permitted. But just as they finished, they heard a loud 'Thar she blows" that was repeated around the ship.

"A whale. They have spotted a whale, Elizabeth. You will get your wish this trip."

Darcy threw back his head and guffawed as his beautiful wife, the perfect example of decorum squealed in delight every bit as much like her sister Lydia.

"Well, come. I must see this whale. Oh, Papa will be so surprised when I tell him what I saw. He might even wish he had come with us."

"Oh, no. This is our trip and our whale."

For a few seconds, the two of them were nearly doubled-over with laughter. Then William grabbed her hand, and they hurried on deck.

"Mrs. Darcy. You are getting your desire to see a whale." Lowery pointed toward the middle of the Irish Sea they traversed until Elizabeth saw the whale at a distance. "Here. Use the spyglass."

"What type of whale is it?"

"Look closely at the plume spray when it exhales from its airhole. Is it straight up, a narrow plume or is it a very wide one?"

"There is nothing for the moment."

"Just wait. When he dives, and then surfaces again, he will exhale."

"Oh, no. He just disappeared."

"Never fear. Keep watching. He will surface again in a few minutes."

Elizabeth waited but was afraid he would never reappear. All this time, the clipper ship was drawing closer to where the whale had been hunting food.

Suddenly, the whale breached and landed with a huge splash. Shortly thereafter, Elizabeth let out a loud "Oh! Now I understand what you mean. The spray is tall, like a column."

"Ah. 'Tis very likely it's a fin whale. When they exhale, the plume of water is tall and narrow like an inverted cone. If it was a humpback whale like Mr. Darcy saw our last trip out, it would be a wide spray. Each whale has a different shaped plume, and that's why they can be identified at a distance. I hear tell of grey whales that have two blowholes, and their plume is heart-shaped. May I see, and I can verify whether or not it is a fin whale."

"Yes, Mrs. Darcy. You have correctly identified a fin whale, one of several whales seen from time to time in the Irish Sea."

"Can we get closer to him?"

"We can get a bit closer to him, Elizabeth, but if we get too close, he will dive and not resurface. So, we do have to be careful."

Lowery gave instructions to get as close as they reasonably could without frightening the whale, so all could get a better look. As the men manned the sails, they took care to stay a little closer to the shoreline hoping that the whale would continue to feed and ignore them. Most had never seen a fin whale before and were just as curious as Elizabeth.

"William, what is that over there?"

"Where?"

"Over where all the green vegetation is."

"Captain, what do we have here?"

"Ah, bloody hell. That's a basking shark. And he shouldn't be here at this time of year."

"Oh, a shark. I never thought we'd see a shark. Oh, Papa is going to be so envious."

"So, what is a basking shark?"

"It's a bloody big shark, nineteen to twenty-six feet in length. But in spite of its size, it is non-aggressive. However, they come here during the warmer months, April through July then leave for warm waters. This one should've already migrated south."

"Why would it stay?"

"Probably for a sad reason, Mrs. Darcy. Perhaps the warmer weather we've had has induced it to stay. Or this may be an old one...or it could be sick. Whatever the reason, it will not survive the winter here. It's not normal for them not to migrate to where it is warmer."

"Such a noble creature to have such an end."

"I agree, ma'am. And please pardon my language. It was a shock to see the basking shark at this time of year."

Elizabeth nodded. "I understand. 'Tis a sad thing to know that death is inevitable."

Lowery did not reply. And all on board were quiet for a time.

***

That night, they dropped anchor at Waterford Port a little after dark. They had very carefully maneuvered up to the dock with very little light, among what looked like several war ships. Since they were here for only one night, the sailors stayed aboard ship and only the Darcys and Lowery stayed at the Inn.

Early to rise the next morning, they again got a very early start, and the weather appeared to be calm and, hopefully, would continue to be without incident. At this time of year, squalls could pop up without warning, and they would need to be careful and prepared. However, the day was entirely uneventful, and Elizabeth slept most of the afternoon. And the only sightings of wildlife were dozens of sea birds including two huge albatrosses over which several sailors bemoaned the bad luck.

"Bad luck? We ain't had no bad luck. And the missus, I believe, brought us good luck. We seen a whale, a shark, and thousands of dolphins. Best trip we ever had."

Grudgingly, the others agreed with him. But the day passed with no major sightings and only the presence of lots of water.

Chapter XVIII

Arriving in Cork, the Darcys obtained the largest suite of rooms in the best hotel in town. The next day William sent an express to his friend, Jonathan Jefferyes of Blarney House, to let him know they had arrived for a stay of a fortnight and that his wife would dearly love to see the inside of Blarney Castle if it was not an imposition.

"William, so you put the blame on me for wanting to see the castle, eh? I thought you wanted to see it as well."

"I do, Elizabeth. However, Jonathan is a bit of a ladies' man, and if he thinks you are the one desiring the tour, he will be more amenable to saying yes."

"Oh, dear. He is not a rake, is he?"

"I understand that he has had a bit of a reputation when he was younger, but he married two years ago and seems to be happy. In fact, it was touted as a love match."

"Ah, and I can relate to a love match also."

And she proceeded to kiss him ardently until there was a knock at the door. The man had a reply from Mr. Jefferyes. William's friend was requesting that they come and stay at Blarney House, tour the castle, and attend a ball they were having in five days.

"Shall we respond favorably, or do you wish to stay here?"

"May we stay here for the next two days and do some shopping and then join your friends?"

"Your wish is my command, my love. I will send a reply that we can join them on Monday, and the ball will be Wednesday night. Perhaps, Tuesday, we could tour the castle and learn its secrets."

So, the Darcys proceeded to break their fast then dress warmly before searching for the best bookshops in town. No matter where he went, William would look for first editions or any book that he wanted to add to Pemberley's massive library. Elizabeth would also be looking for ones that her father would appreciate as well.

They had been walking the crowded streets of Cork for just a short while when Darcy stopped, looked at someone across the street and several shops away, and muttered a curse that surprised his wife.

"Follow my lead, Elizabeth."

He then grabbed his wife's elbow and pushed her in another direction from where they had been walking. Moving quickly, he steered her into an alley then grasped her hand and quietly ordered her to run.

As they sprinted down the alleyway, he removed his tall beaver hat and tossed it into a rubbish bin behind one of the shops. Elizabeth's mouth dropped open, and she started to question their mad dash but stayed quiet instead and decided that her husband knew what he was doing.

Still running, he led them between two buildings, across a street then into another alley. Finding a deep doorway, Darcy pushed Elizabeth into it and whispered, "Trust me, sweetheart." Elizabeth found herself assaulted by her husband's lips and hands, and her eyes got as big as saucers.

"Any idee where they went?"

"No, just keep looking."

The two men who had been searching for them appeared at the end of the alley as William turned slightly to hide his wife from their view. As the men came near, they saw what the couple was doing and guffawed.

"Hey, Benji. Will ye look at that."

The two rough-looking characters continued to snicker and make ribald comments as Darcy began lifting Elizabeth's skirt with one hand as his wife blushed to her toes. With his other hand, he waved the men away while he and Elizabeth ardently hoped they would get the message and leave.

But, they did not.

"Benji. I recognize that fancy hat she's wearin.' That's them we been chasin'."

"Aye, ye got a good eye for details."

"Ye need to come with us. There somebody wantin' to see ye."

Darcy saw that the men were only carrying knives. Neither had a gun, and that gave him an advantage. At the same time he spun toward the men, he thrust his cane-sword toward Elizabeth, pulled a small dagger from his boot, and buried it in the arm of the first man who had spoken. With his other hand, he pulled a small pistol from his coat pocket while Elizabeth released the cane's sword.

The first man screamed when hit with the dagger, and the man called Benji laughed at Darcy's pistol.

"And what you goin' to do with that little pop gun?"

"Do you really want to know?" Darcy smiled at Benji, and the man laughed.

"Aye. I want to know."

"It seems that because I do a lot of target practice that I am quite a good marksman with either hand. All I have to do is put a bullet in your eye and you are a dead man."

Benji's smirk rapidly vanished.

"Benji, I gotta see someone so I don't bleed to death."

"Shut up. You ain't gonna bleed to death."

"Well, *gentlemen,* I believe we are at an impasse."

At the quizzical looks on the faces of the two men, Darcy explained, "That means a stalemate. No winner." He smiled again at the two men. "I suggest you leave and never come near us again."

And without another word from Benji and only mutterings from his friend, they left. Their orders were to capture the Darcys, not get killed.

As soon as they were out of sight, Darcy took hold of Elizabeth's hand again and, moving at a fast pace, lead her in such a manner through the streets and alleyways as to discourage any trackers.

"William, what is happening?"

"I'll explain as soon as we get back to the hotel."

And to his wife's surprise, he took a circular route to the back of the building, took them through the hotel's kitchen, which shocked and dismayed the workers, and then went up the servants' stairway to the upper floors. Reaching their rooms, he unlocked the door, ushered Elizabeth quickly into the room then relocked the door. It was then that he sighed in relief.

"William."

Sitting down in a beautifully upholstered chair, he pulled Elizabeth onto his lap and held her close without saying a word. She smiled at him and placed her hands on either side of his face just prior to gently kissing him. Elizabeth could feel him shaking but didn't know if it was because he was scared, possibly for her, or if he was angry.

It turned out that he was both. One name sufficed. "Wickham."

"I thought Wickham and Denny went to America."

"So, did I. Mrs. Younge actually saw them get on the ship. I have no idea how they wound up in Cork."

"How do you know this involves Mr. Wickham?"

"I saw him."

"Oh! Where was he?"

"He and the two men who chased us were across the street and three shops away right before we ran. He said something to them and then pointed to us. When they started to move quickly toward us, that is when I had you run. I am sorry, Elizabeth. Are you well? All I could think of was to protect you by getting you away from them as fast as possible."

"Yes, I am well. A little breathless for a few minutes, but I am well because of my wonderful husband who is not only very intelligent and very much in love with me—much to my delight—he is also a marvelous strategist in outwitting men with wicked intent."

"And I will continue to the best of my ability. I love you, Elizabeth, and would give my life to protect you."

"Let us hope that does not become necessary."

"I agree. But for now, I believe we need to leave Cork and join my friend and his family."

"But would Wickham endanger them also?"

"Jonathan is very protective of his family and his property. If we stayed in Cork, we would have to stay indoors at the hotel the entire time. At least at Blarney House, we can be a little freer. He does have men who protect all he has because several years ago, they were threatened by a family seeking vengeance for a former relative's actions. So, we should be safe there."

"Goodness gracious. What had the relative done?"

"Jonathan never found out, but he never quit having his property, including the castle, guarded."

"What do you think Wickham was trying to accomplish?"

"Kidnapping. By holding us for ransom, especially you, he would be demanding a large sum of money and get vengeance on me as well. He's never forgiven me for the failed elopement at Ramsgate. He needed Georgiana's dowry badly as he had many debts of honor he owed. They did not kill him, but they broke his arm and one leg. He was never as strong after that."

"What will we do?"

"Ring for the maid and send a note to the manager. I will request he get a carriage and eight armed outriders for our trip to Blarney House. It is only about five miles away from Cork. We should not have any problems…I hope."

The next morning, Darcy had their trunks loaded onto the carriage, but he made no arrangements for foot warmers as the distance was not long. And he prepared two pistols that would be in the carriage with him and Elizabeth just in case of trouble. He knew if Wickham was desperate, he would try again.

Chapter XIX

"Are you ready, my dear?"

"Yes, and I look forward to meeting your friends. So far, your friends have been very interesting people," she said with a smile. And because she couldn't resist, she gave him another kiss and melted in his arms. "Mmm, I love to be kissed by you."

"Surely, there is no one else."

"Never, William. You will always be the only one for me."

Holding Elizabeth close for another minute or so, he finally let her go with a sigh. "We do need to get started. Jonathan is expecting us before luncheon."

Before leaving the hotel, Darcy took a moment to look out the main window to see if he could spot Wickham. He hoped he was wrong and that the man had given up. But he knew his childhood friend and how tenacious he could be when pursuing an objective, generally one that would serve him ill. *If he had only applied that tenacity to pursuing something worthwhile.*

Soon they were on their way and had been traveling but little over a quarter hour when the coach lurched, and they were nearly thrown to the floor.

"Elizabeth, are you well?"

"Yes, what's happening?"

Shots were fired, and Darcy shoved his wife to the floor, grateful he had left the bottom of the coach empty on impulse. Afraid the coach would wreck, especially if the driver was shot, Darcy stretched out over Elizabeth to give her as much protection as he was able.

For several minutes gunfire rang out until suddenly the coach was brought to a halt and silence descended. Waiting a moment, then cautiously raising his head, Darcy was shocked speechless at the bullet hole where his beloved wife's head would have been if he hadn't acted quickly. Saying a quick prayer of thanksgiving, he called out. "Is everyone well?"

Clambering from the coach after ascertaining Elizabeth was in no danger, he promised to return as soon as he determined the damage.

Six of the outriders appeared, and the leader apprised Darcy of what had transpired.

"Mr. Darcy, sir, the blackguards are either dead, dying, or captured. One of my men is injured and needs attention as well as one of the prisoners. Shall I send for the magistrate?"

"Yes, please, and have him bring someone to tend to the injured also."

"Mr. Darcy, Holmes is seriously injured too."

"Have you been able to stop the bleeding?"

"Yes, sir, for the moment. Had no idee he would be shot instead of drivin' this day.

Darcy was glad Elizabeth was doing well and he could concentrate on the men. Having three men, one outrider, a prisoner, and the spare coachman injured made a beautiful day ugly instead. He would be glad when he and Elizabeth would finally arrive at Blarney House and put this behind them.

Hearing hoof beats, he turned and saw the prisoners the outriders had taken. Three men had their heads hanging down as they were prevented escaping by the pistols pointed at them. None of them was Wickham.

"Let me have one of your horses and take me to the dead and dying."

Pointing to one of the outriders, who immediately relinquished his horse to Darcy, he and the leader were soon on their way back to where they came from. Four bodies were scattered over a quarter kilometer. After determining that one dead body was Denny, Darcy went looking for Wickham and found him. He was not dead…yet.

Kneeling down by his former friend, who was seriously injured with a shot to the chest, Darcy asked him 'why.'

Coughing, Wickham replied, "Why…not. You had everything, and I had nothing. I've always wanted what you had: looks, money, prestige, power." Spitting up a little blood, he continued with effort. "And when we were…abandoned here by the captain, we lived…as we could. By our wits."

"Do not talk. We are getting someone to help with injuries."

"No, I will talk…while…I…can. Seems I…will…escape the hangman's…noose after all." Wickham grimaced and continued. "But…all your fault. Blasted farmer and his wife. He…didn't…like cuckold, and he…."

"He did what, George?"

"He stole…my…manhood."

Darcy just shook his head. Learning his enemy had been castrated didn't surprise him. The man was forever seducing women from one end of England to the other, whether single or married mattered not. It seemed though that the Irish were even less tolerant of his proclivities, and the farmer had taken retribution for Wickham having slept with his wife. And, now, every bad deed that Wickham had perpetrated down through the years had caught up with him at last.

"And you…stole…Elizabeth, the only…one I ever loved." With a look of pure hatred on his face, his former friend drew his last breath.

For a moment, Darcy couldn't believe he was dead. The shock of seeing someone he knew dying in front of him caused the back of his eyes to prick and his heart to clench. Reaching down he closed Wickham's eyes then sat back on his heels.

"Mister Darcy, are ye well?"

Darcy couldn't speak yet, but he nodded his head.

Satisfied, the outrider proceeded to help the others bring the injured man and the dead bodies to where the coach had halted and the prisoners were waiting. Elizabeth bolted out of the coach the minute Darcy appeared, and he immediately held her close as she cried and the other men looked away.

"All is well, my love. Denny and Wickham both are dead, and the rest are prisoners. The magistrate will be here shortly, and soon we can be on our way."

With tears running down her face, she replied, "It may be settled legally, but we will never forget this day. I cannot believe Mr. Wickham and Mr. Denny are dead. I have never had anyone I know die before. In spite of their wickedness, I feel my heart breaking."

"Beloved, it has more to do with death itself than the men who died. Death is very hurtful especially when we lose loved ones. The loss is final and is painful."

He had dealt with death before. First, it was his grandparents, then his mother followed by his father. He knew exactly how difficult death was to deal with. He would have to be of a great comfort to his wife over the next few days and even the next few months. *If nothing else happens, perhaps we can weather the storm of our emotions and be of solace to each other.*

***

Three hours later, they arrived at Blarney House, and after introductions, Darcy asked Elizabeth if she needed to rest a short while before luncheon.

"Yes, please. I hate to seem an ungrateful guest, but it has been a tragic morning"

"Think nothing of it, my dear Mrs. Darcy. What a terrible thing to have happen to you. I cannot imagine such an occurrence. Of course, you may rest a while. And if you need to sleep a bit, we will manage and see you at tea or dinner."

"Thank you, Mrs. Jefferyes."

"Please call me Abigail."

"And I am Elizabeth."

The housekeeper showed them to their suite of rooms, and Darcy took his wife in his arms as soon as the woman had departed.

"Are you well, my love?"

This was one of those times that a husband wished he had said nothing. His inquiry opened the gates to a torrent of tears as his beautiful wife broke down and cried with great gulping sobs as he held her close and rubbed her back. He felt his own eyes smart at the memory of the horrible morning as well.

After a while, Elizabeth's tears slowed, and she gulped and apologized. "I am sorry, William, to be such a watering pot."

"Shhh, beloved. You have nothing to be ashamed of or to apologize for. It is a horrific thing to be attacked not knowing why or what would happen. I have even seen grown men break down under trying circumstances that threaten life and limb."

"Oh, I thought that I might just be a silly woman for it affecting me so. Mr. Wickham…."

"I know. He *was* a friend when I was growing up, ever since we were in leading strings. A good friend. He and I were there for each other until he noticed women. My father never understood that even the maids at Pemberley were not safe from him, but they were afraid of losing their position if they complained. Two were sent away when they became *enceinte* although they would never say who the father was. Those were times when George just smirked and continued his profligate ways. At Cambridge it was even worse, as I mentioned before. Too unspeakable to share with you, a genteel woman. His gambling, drinking, and chasing every woman in sight was cause for me to find other rooms. But his exploits were the talk of Cambridge. He was not pleased when I gave him the cut direct. And Bingley did the same. To this day, he just seemed to add to his sins. I had hoped…."

The two cuddled for a while until Elizabeth fell asleep. Darcy pulled down the covers then undressed his wife down to her chemise and gently laid her on the bed. Then he did the same for himself and crawled under the blankets and pulled his wife to him. Both slept the afternoon away and awoke only when the housekeeper tapped on the door. Dinner was to be served within an hour.

Chapter XX

Rather than insult their hosts, the Darcys refreshed themselves and changed into proper attire for dining. And they were glad they did. The Jefferyes set a delightful table, and the food was delicious. Elizabeth found that she could try a bit of every course since she had had nothing to eat since that morning. Sleeping through luncheon and tea guaranteed that the couple had hearty appetites come evening.

The company was interesting as well. Because the ball would be held in two days, three couples who had traveled some distance were staying at Blarney House for the next week. Mr. and Mrs. Byrne had come over twenty-five miles to attend the ball and visit with their cousins, the Jefferyes. Mr. O'Neill was a business associate of Sir Jonathan's as was Darcy and Mr. Kelly. The four men were all investors in the clipper ships and had done very well for themselves. When the ladies left the men to their port and cigars, the talk was mostly about the attack on the Darcys that morning which was the last topic Darcy wished to speak of.

The ladies would have had the same discussion as the men except that Abigail, in regard to Elizabeth's feelings, would not allow it and suggested that they have a little entertainment from those proficient on the pianoforte.

"Elizabeth, we will excuse you this evening, but I hope that we may hear you play and sing before the week is out."

Elizabeth blushed and demurred. "I do play but very ill, however, my singing voice is a little better."

"I'm sure it's delightful. Perhaps tomorrow night we may impose on you to sing and play for us."

"Perhaps."

"In the meantime, Mrs. Byrne, would you indulge us this evening, please?"

"Of course. Would you prefer something light such as Mozart, or would Herr Beethoven be your choice?"

As it occurred, the ladies asked for both, and as the last few notes of Mozart's Minuet in G Major were played after the Beethoven piece, the men joined them. Business would be discussed another day. This evening they wished to be with their ladies and enjoy the entertainment which continued for a little while longer than the Darcys preferred.

"Elizabeth, are you ready to retire? You are quieter than usual."

"Oh, do you imply that I am a chatterbox?" she teased.

"Never, my dear. However, it has been a difficult day. Perhaps a good night's sleep would leave you refreshed on the morrow."

"I believe that you are correct. I do feel a bit like I stayed up half the night which was certainly not the case. The events of the day have left me a bit exhausted."

"Jonathan, Abigail, would you please excuse us. It has been a rather trying day. But we will say that dinner was delicious, and the company was delightful. We have enjoyed meeting everyone and look forward to the ball and the rest of our visit."

Darcy bowed, and Elizabeth curtseyed to their hosts, and they bid all goodnight and headed to their bedchambers. As usual, Darcy slept with his wife and the two were comforted with just holding one another and grateful that neither had been injured in the catastrophic events of that morning. Hopefully, that would be the only time they would experience such a terrible incident.

***

The next morning, Elizabeth awoke with a headache. This was not an unusual occurrence as she was prone to them when under stress. And, although they were due to tour Blarney Castle, it turned out that the weather was not going to cooperate. Clouds laden with moisture had moved in during the night, and heavy rainfall woke them both.

"Elizabeth, are you well?"

"No. My head hurts. Yesterday was much too stressful, and my body is rebelling."

"Go back to sleep, my love. The rain has dampened any plans to see the castle or to even take a walk on the grounds. It is a perfect day to rest and recuperate. You must feel well on the morrow as the ball is tomorrow night, and there will be over one hundred guests attending."

Even when they had been at dinner the night before, the quick movements of the servants showed that they were taking seriously preparations for the ball. Jonathan and Abigail held two balls per year: one in November prior to the holidays and one in the spring just before the summer months began. In this part of Ireland, the Jefferyes ball was a major event.

So, Elizabeth took William's words to heart and went back to sleep for most of the day. And when she finally arose, she did not have a headache, and she felt very refreshed. Enough so that she spent some quality time with her husband after telling the maid she wouldn't be needed until before dinner when Elizabeth required her hair being styled. Knowing they would not be interrupted, they showed their love to one another and gained comfort after the events of the day before.

That evening they very much enjoyed the entertainment, and Elizabeth even offered to sing and play a couple of songs that were welcomed heartily. She wasn't as proficient as Georgiana, but she played with enthusiasm and with her heart which was greatly appreciated by her husband and the other guests. Again, it was a delightful evening.

***

"Would you like something to eat, Elizabeth? It will be a good while before the supper dance, and you ate very little when we had tea."

"I suppose I should. I probably will be ravenous after dancing all evening on an empty stomach. A couple of sandwiches and some more tea would be lovely."

When the light fare, coffee, and tea were brought, Elizabeth tucked into her food as if she had not eaten for a week. Her husband just smiled. Her need for sleep, her appetite fluctuating, and her emotions moving from happiness to sadness at a moment's notice had convinced him she was with child. Before Georgiana was born, the doctor had said that the symptoms of Lady Anne being *enceinte* were too early to be showing, but he was proved wrong when she delivered Darcy's beautiful sister almost eight months later. *And Elizabeth is showing the same symptoms early as well. She must be with child.* Darcy could feel his chest swell with pride and never doubted she would give birth to a child nine months after their wedding night. *Will it be my heir or a miniature Elizabeth? I care not as long as the babe is healthy and Elizabeth is well.*

***

Darcy suppressed a gasp of pleasure at seeing the vision of loveliness his wife presented to him. Her gown of deep green silk complimented the dark brown of her hair with its red highlights. The modiste had trimmed it with a modest amount of lace that had been accentuated with pearls that were repeated on the silk ribbon that was threaded through her abundant curls. Her skirt had a sheer overlay of slightly lighter green that shifted color in the glow of the candles and made her look like a fairy princess. *My princess.*

He whispered, "Elizabeth." No other words were needed as he took her face gently in his hands and kissed her with all the passion that was in his heart.

When he let her go, and Elizabeth caught her breath, she sighed. "Mr. Darcy, I fear if we do this again, we shall never make it to the ball."

"I care not for the ball. You know how I feel about dancing. The only one I wish to dance with is you. And staying here and having the pleasure of undressing…"

"Oh, no," she said playfully. "We have obligations this evening. Misters Byrne, Kelly, and O'Neill have already requested dances as well as Sir Jonathan. But never fear, I told them the first and the supper dances were already taken by my husband."

"Elizabeth. I want the last dance also."

She saw the gleam in his eye and knew when the ball was over, the aftermath would be the best part.

"Come, Mr. Darcy. I look forward to the evening and dancing with my husband, and I hope the last dance does not cause a scandal when I dance my third with you."

She gave him a smile that was full of promise, and he sighed and bowed to the inevitable: an evening dancing with the other wives. Then he smirked when he contemplated the three dances with his beloved wife. Dancing with Elizabeth was different. It was like being in heaven, and he would tolerate the rest of the evening to have that time with her.

She placed her hand over his extended one, so he could escort her to the ballroom. Elizabeth would have rather placed it around his elbow and snuggled up to him, but it would wrinkle her dress, and that wouldn't do even before the dancing began.

As they appeared at the top of the stairs, Sir Jonathan and the other three men clapped as they came down the stairs. Elizabeth could feel her face warm, and William knew the tips of his ears were pink.

Abigail approached and said, "Elizabeth, you look lovely. You will be the envy of all the ladies at the ball."

"Oh, I sincerely hope not. I would not wish for my husband to be calling every man out for the morrow."

Her hostess giggled then replied, "Surely Mr. Darcy can allow the men one night to admire such a beautiful lady. No?"

"They may look but not touch except for the dancing." He had such a stern look on his face that Abigail almost thought him serious in his comments. She didn't know him well enough to be aware that he was extremely serious and very protective of Elizabeth.

"May you both have a lovely evening and enjoy the supper. The cooks have outdone themselves in preparing a most delicious meal." Then she left to join Sir Jonathan in the receiving line.

Darcy sighed. *I must remember to keep my mind on the dancing and not worry about Elizabeth.* He smirked as he thought of his intelligent wife and knew that if any man on the property did not comport himself as a gentleman that she was more than capable of giving him a setdown and putting him in his place. Finally, he began to relax and was determined to enjoy the evening.

***

Elizabeth discovered by the second one that all her dances had been taken, and she was dancing with Mr. Byrne prior to the supper dance, when he made an indecent proposal to her. Elizabeth hesitated only a moment.

When the dance allowed her to speak with him again, she smiled and commented, "How unfortunate for you, Mr. Byrne, that my husband is a jealous man. Just before we were married, he called a man out that insulted me and would have killed him had I not mentioned the imprudence of him doing so. That was the fourth time he has met someone on the field of honor. Mr. Darcy is a *very* honorable man…and he is an extremely good shot as well as swordsman. I would hate for your wife to become a widow so soon." All this was said quietly as if they were having a normal conversation.

Byrne blanched and debated abandoning her on the floor but thought her husband would take that as an insult and definitely call him out. So, he staunchly finished the dance with her, escorted her to Darcy, mumbled a thank you, and nearly ran from her presence. Elizabeth was delighted he never approached her again.

"My dear, you look like the cat that ate the cream. Might I inquire as to why?"

"'Tis nothing, William. Simply a ladies' joke," she said with a smile.

"Ah." And he was satisfied with that, much to her relief.

The rest of the evening went well, supper was wonderful, and they enjoyed the last dance knowing what awaited them when they went back to their suite.

***

Later, with their passion sated, they slept until William was awakened with Elizabeth crying.

"Beloved, what is wrong?"

When she could finally speak, with a hiccup she related the nightmare she had just dreamed.

"It was dreadful. I dreamed of Wickham attacking us again, but this time he killed you and forced me to go with him without caring for your body. It tore me apart to leave you." And she broke down crying again.

William held her close and rocked her until she fell again into a troubled sleep. He lay awake the rest of the night until well after dawn holding her tightly to him. *Will she be well? Should we stay or return home to Pemberley?* He would quiz her later and see what she wanted. He would do anything to keep her happy.

Chapter XXI

Although the day was fair and the wind mild, William chose to stay indoors with Elizabeth. She had had no more nightmares, but she slept poorly. He watched over her all afternoon and nodded off a time or two himself. But he would always wake when she stirred.

"William, what is the hour? Did I miss tea?"

"No matter, my love. Are you hungry? The last time you ate was at the ball."

"Yes, I am a little bit hungry. Could you have them bring some tea and sandwiches and maybe a piece or two of fruit?"

"'Twould be my pleasure. Do you wish to dress, or should I bring your robe?"

"My robe, please."

Elizabeth disappeared into the water closet, and when she returned, she washed her face even though the water was cold. William started when she heaved a great sigh.

"Are you unwell?"

"I am better. Thankfully, I had no more nightmares. I did sleep somewhat easy. Perhaps it was something I ate."

"I am doubtful of that. The incident the other morning will probably stay with us for a while until time erases it. Life-threatening occurrences are not very forgettable. I just wish I could have prevented it."

"Perhaps it is just as well you did not. I fear Wickham would have been in and out of our lives for years if he were still living. I might have been afraid every day of my life if that was so. As it is, with him dead, we are free of his machinations for the rest of our lives. I cannot regret that. No, 'tis better this way. And one day, I will forget."

Motioning to her, William took her on his lap, mindful that the maid would be returning soon with their repast. Holding her close and gently kissing her hair, her forehead, and her hand, he repeated, "I love you, Elizabeth," as she clung to him for dear life. They had about a quarter hour until there was a knock at the door.

"A moment, please."

Elizabeth reluctantly arose and sat in a nearby chair as William answered the door and showed the maid where to set the tray down. Then thanking her, he watched as she exited and closed the door.

Taking Elizabeth's hand, he gave thanks audibly, and in his heart, he gave thanks again that they both had survived Wickham's attack. *If he had had more men to back him up, he might have been successful*, and William shivered at the thought.

"William?"

He shook his head. "I am well. Never fear, Elizabeth. I am always here for you."

She smiled and handed him a cup of coffee, but she appreciated his attempt to lift her spirits. *I chose well when I accepted his hand in marriage. There will never be another like him.*

She laughed, just as he desired her to, when he waggled his eyebrows at her.

"Are you missing your family?"

"Yes, and I especially miss Jane and Papa. Jane and I have not been able to write directly to each other since coming here as we knew not where we would be. So, I look forward to a pile of letters from her when we get home."

"You mean…Pemberley?"

"Of course, silly man. Pemberley is my home now. And quite lovely it is. I am just a little intimidated at becoming mistress of such great an estate. I hope Mrs. Reynolds can bring me up to snuff rapidly, so things will continue running smoothly."

"I have no doubts you will do well. The servants are already willing to stand with my wife, and as amenable as you are and considerate of everyone, no matter their station, they will accept you without question. After all, I chose you." With that proud comment, he puffed out his chest and nodded.

With raised eyebrows, his wife responded, "Oh, no. *I* chose to accept you when you offered for me."

A passing maid startled at the laughter that emanated from the Darcys' suite. But having heard that they were recently married, she could not help but smile.

***

Later, they dressed for dinner, and Elizabeth found herself seated next to Mr. Byrne who took great pains to ignore her and speak only with Mrs. Kelly with whom he had nothing in common. Elizabeth was hard pressed to not dissolve in laughter as she caught occasional comments from one of the two.

However, Sir Jonathan was to the right of her, and they had pleasant converse for the majority of the meal. Elizabeth had shown interest in his family history, and that opened the floodgates of information concerning Blarney castle and the former owners, one of which was Donough MacCarty, who was made 1st Earl of Clancarty.

"And when did your family acquire the castle?"

"My grandfather, Sir James St. John Jefferyes, who was the governor of Cork City at that time, purchased it in the early 1700's. Sometime later, my family built this house where we have lived ever since."

"And it is a very beautiful home, Sir Jonathan. There is quite a history in connection with the castle, and I am looking forward to touring it when we can."

"If it does not rain tomorrow, I will make arrangement for all the guests to see our pride and joy. We even have a special stone with a history of its own that I will tell about."

"I look forward to it, and thank you, Sir."

The evening also turned out to be the most enjoyable as most of the ladies played and sang. And Lady Jefferyes even played the harp to the pleasure of all.

At the end of the evening, Sir Jonathan made an announcement about touring the castle on the morrow, and there were ooh's and aah's as they all looked forward to seeing the inside of one of these bastions of defense. Then the group dispersed for the evening with Byrne hurrying ahead with his wife, so he would not encounter the Darcys. Darcy looked quizzical, and Elizabeth merely shrugged, and then it was forgotten.

***

The next morning saw sunny skies and cool temperatures. However, the guests were not going to let that deter them. They dressed warmly and trooped out the entrance of Blarney House and headed toward the castle a short distance away.

As they approached the large fortress, Sir Jonathan began describing the various defenses of the castle.

"The large mounds of earth and rocks around the castle are called ramparts. Since the major reason castles were built was for defense, this is Blarney Castle's first line of defense."

"Are not most castles surrounded by a moat?"

"That they are, Mrs. Darcy. Most castles are built near rivers for that very reason. However, Blarney castle is too far from water, so the builders' option was for ramparts instead. Scaling them would not only take much effort, the besiegers would be getting fatigued by the time they were ready to storm the castle."

"The ramparts were a wise choice for the defenders then."

"Yes, they were, but they were not the only defense. Each castle has several lines of defense; some on the outside, others on the inside."

"I look forward to seeing some of these other features."

Sir Jonathan smiled at Elizabeth and placed her hand around his elbow before Darcy realized his intention and said, "Mrs. Darcy, I would be pleased to show you…and the other guests some of these other defenses."

Darcy raised his hand to object and Abigail Jefferyes laughed. "Mr. Darcy, my husband is just having a little fun at your expense. His real objective is bragging about his castle to anyone but especially a beautiful lady such as your wife. I trust him implicitly, and you will find that you can as well. I fear he is a bit of a show-off like a little boy displaying his favorite toy. Your wife is the first one who indicated real interest, and that is why he has taken her under

149

his wing. She will be his protégé for the next little while until I ask him a question, and then I will be put on his arm, and you will have your wife back. In fact, if you had asked a question first, you would have become his protégé for the day."

Darcy just rolled his eyes and continued to watch Sir Jonathan. In a few minutes, Lady Jefferyes asked a question of her husband, and he immediately abandoned Elizabeth and reached for his wife's hand. And Darcy took back his wife with relief.

After showing the guest the portcullis, a metal grillwork that slid down and blocked the doorway, all entered the castle. Every guest appreciated that they had not been required to climb the ramparts as a dirt ramp had been made so they were able to walk right to the castle doorway. Inside, Sir Jonathan proceeded to show them the murder holes, the purpose of which was to allow defenders to pour boiling water or oil down on anyone who breached the castle. While he was giving them more information about how the castle could be defended, William took Elizabeth a little further in to a large stairway.

"Elizabeth, what is the first thing that you notice about the staircase?"

"It is built in a spiral. Do you know why?"

"Can you guess why?"

"Everything about the castle involves the defense of it. I gather that this is also one of those defensive measures."

"I knew you were an intelligent woman. And you just won fifty kisses."

Elizabeth smiled. "But why in a clockwise spiral? What would be the advantage?"

"For defending the castle. Most people favor their right hand. Defenders of the castle would need to be able to freely swing their swords against besiegers. And they found by making the staircase in this fashion, their enemies would have difficulties wielding their swords coming up the stairs as they would find their right sides against the interior curve of the wall."

"And the defenders would not have that problem as they would be coming down the staircase and could swing their swords without difficulty."

"Correct you are. I love that I have a most intelligent wife, and I will enjoy surrendering those fifty kisses to you."

"Will you now?" And the gleam of desire in his eyes sent a frisson of delight down her spine.

"Yes, I will," he growled and snugged her close to his side.

Turning toward the other guests, they heard Sir Jonathan speaking about the Blarney Stone and listened with avid interest.

After telling about the legend of kissing the stone and receiving the ability to speak the gift of the gab or with eloquence without offense, Sir Jonathan invited his guests to walk to the top of the castle to kiss the stone.

"Sir Jonathan, the castle is nearly 82 feet high. The men might be willing to climb that far, but I and the rest of the ladies would find that too much of a climb."

"Mrs. Darcy, how did you know how tall the castle is?"

Elizabeth blushed to find herself the object of attention…again. "Clearing her throat, she said," I have helped my father around Longbourn, particularly with his ledgers and the various buildings on the property. I am particularly fond of working with numbers and my father always had me do calculations for him as he found no pleasure in them. And he taught me how to determine the dimensions of the new barn we had built two years ago. I have found since then that I seem to know immediately the approximate height of any structure or even a hill fairly quickly."

"Do you mean to say I married a mathematical genius?" William whispered.

"Shhh. I do not wish that bandied about."

He raised both hands in surrender. "I am delighted. There are times when I am fatigued that numbers confound me for a while. I am more than willing to put them in the capable hands of my wife."

"William," she hissed.

He chuckled as he could not keep a straight face when teasing her, and Elizabeth was pleased that he was learning to be more relaxed when with others and to enjoy a little banter with her as well. She would be sure to make it worth his while when they returned to their suite of rooms.

In the meantime, all the guests had decided that making that huge climb to the top of the castle was not worth it just to look at a rock, and they headed back to Blarney House after finding out how the battlements on top, that could be seen from the ground, were used for defense. All in all, they were pleased with the experience and had found the castle interesting.

All except Mr. Byrne who kept as far away from the Darcys as he possibly could. Elizabeth pretended not to notice that his wife kept tugging on his arm and speaking to him in a low voice as they walked away from the castle. She had to hide her smirk as she felt he had earned it.

***

When they arrived back at their suite, Darcy began immediately giving his kisses away to Elizabeth until she asked, "May we converse for a few minutes?"

"Certainly, Elizabeth. What concerns you?"

"I have enjoyed most of our trip, particularly our time in Dublin. I also feel that if Wickham had never showed, the portion of our time here would have been just as enjoyable. But I find that my heart is just not in it. What I would like to do is go back to Cork and find the book shops we were not able to search for. Do a little shopping on the morrow, especially for first editions, attend church on Sunday, and begin the return to Liverpool on Monday. I believe I am ready to go home…to Pemberley if you agree."

"Certainly, I agree. I just need to be with you wherever you are. I will go speak with Sir Jonathan now if it pleases you."

"It pleases me, beloved, and assure him that we find no fault with him or Abigail. It is just that…everything has been a bit much. And I want to see home and Georgiana and even Mrs. Reynolds and the rest of the servants. And Cousin Richard also."

"Come, Elizabeth. Sit a moment." And William patted his lap. Elizabeth couldn't resist. It was definitely her most favorite place in the world, on his lap and in his arms. And she sighed contentedly.

A short while later, he found Sir Jonathan and explained that they had enjoyed their hospitality very much but desired to prepare for the journey back to England and Derbyshire. Mentioning again concerning the incident with Wickham, he convinced his host that he was doing what was best for his wife, and Jonathan agreed. Calling for his wife, Abigail showed up a few minutes later and sided with her husband.

"Mr. Darcy, we like your wife very much. You are a very lucky man to have found such a wonderful woman. But we understand that the trauma of nearly being kidnapped or killed can make life difficult for a person, and we would not want to add any burden to Elizabeth. Will you be staying for tonight or did you plan to leave this afternoon?"

"If it's agreeable, we will return to Cork on the morrow if you would help us make arrangements for a coach and outriders for tomorrow morning."

"Not a problem, Darcy. We can have an express sent immediately and have them here early if that is your wish."

"If it would please you, perhaps they could arrive after we have broken our fast."

"Splendid! I will see to it immediately."

Darcy thanked him and went back to tell Elizabeth the news.

Chapter XXII

By Monday morning, all had been cared for. They had found two first editions: one for Pemberley's library and one for Mr. Bennet. The ship was ready and everyone and every necessary item was on board at the crack of dawn. For the moment, the weather was calm and pointed toward a good trip and, it was hoped, a safe trip also.

As they weighed anchor, Elizabeth stood at the rail in awe of all the ships that had appeared after their initial arrival. Not only were there many more ships, she was amazed at some of the war ships, their sizes and their armaments. And it made her a little sad too that mankind still wouldn't work for peace. How she yearned for wars to cease but determined that it was probably just a pipe dream. She was grateful that William was not nor ever had served in the military, but she knew that he worried about Richard. His cousin had recuperated from his wound and should always be in a position to train young pups in the ways of war rather than being on the battlefield, but that was not a surety. If necessary he could still be sent to the battlefield if his rank was high enough, not to fight but to oversee and give orders to those who would be fighting. But it would be no guarantee for his safety as officers were often targeted even though at a distance from the fighting. William had been trying for two years to get Richard to retire and take up ownership of a small estate that her husband was holding for him. It wouldn't make Richard rich but with 2,000 pounds per year, he would live comfortably and could consider marrying for love rather than money.

"What are you thinking of, Elizabeth?"

"Richard and hoping that his prospects will continue to keep him near London and not the Continent."

"I hope the same."

That day there was relatively little to see but water. Seabirds had been near the Port of Cork scavenging for scraps, but few were visible once they drew away from the port and headed to Waterford for the night. Since there was little of interest, Elizabeth and William stayed in the Captain's cabin and read some of the new books they had purchased for pleasure.

Arriving at Waterford, they had an early dinner and retired for the evening as they wished to get a restful night's sleep as the last leg of their trip would take a little bit longer than their trip from Dublin to Cork. This would be because they would be sailing around Holy Head Island—a portion of Wales that jutted out southwest of Liverpool—before they would be changing direction and then heading east to eventually dock at the port.

The Darcys woke up eager to set sail. By the end of the day, they would be just that much closer to home. Both looked forward to seeing Pemberley again.

"Home. It has such a lovely ring to it."

"I agree, love. Georgiana will be delighted to see us again and hearing about Ireland. Richard might even have leave and be waiting for us as well although we have been gone a little less than four weeks."

"It will be good to see them both. I have missed them. Our cousin's sense of humor always makes me smile."

"I too until I am the object of his humor."

Elizabeth giggled at her husband's huff. She was well aware that Richard poked and prodded at William to prevent him from being such a stodgy, hidebound gentleman and to get him to smile more. And Richard's ways usually worked, and he would him laughing in a short while. *William has so many responsibilities. If he would only smile and enjoy life more, I feel he would be able to bear them better.*

Her husband looked questioningly at her wondering why she suddenly seemed more serious, but Elizabeth gave him a brilliant smile that took his breath away and let him know that all was well.

It was only a couple of hours into the ten to twelve hours to Liverpool that clouds began to form. Captain Lowery and Darcy wondered if they would cause problems before the day was over. Most of them seemed to be forming north of them where they would expect to see Holy Head Island, which they had to pass by in about five more hours.

"Mr. Darcy, I don't know if this means trouble or not. They seem to be forming slowly, and they may be just gathering moisture to drop during the night or on the morrow. If it's building up to a storm though, we could be in trouble if we're caught in the open water. We can keep an eye on it and head to shore and drop anchor if it looks too dangerous or we can continue on. If we need to, we can stop at any one of numerous fishing villages all along the coast and wait until the morrow."

"Does it look dangerous right now?"

"No, but it can change in a heartbeat. If it does get bad, my men and I are prepared for it. But I worry about Mrs. Darcy. If it is a storm, the winds can get mighty high and dangerous. The men will even have problems staying on their feet."

"What could I do to protect my wife?"

"There is rope in the closet of my cabin. You can tie the both of you, one on either side of the pole in the middle of the cabin. Tie it with the knot I showed you that holds tight but can be released quickly when you pull the end. You and Mrs. Darcy would need to hug the pole tight and not let the motion of the ship snap your heads into the pole. Do you understand?"

"Yes, I'm going to get the rope out and be prepared. Will we have any warning if the winds increase?"

"Generally, yes. However, if it is a squall, the winds can increase rapidly and are extremely dangerous. If need be, I will send you below if I think you and the missus should tie yourselves to the post. And, Darcy, you will need to do so immediately when I tell you."

"Yes, Captain Lowery." Darcy had no intention of questioning the captain if their lives were in jeopardy. He would do whatever was necessary to protect Elizabeth.

For the next few hours, they watched as the clouds slowly built up in the north. As they got closer, they could that the layers of clouds had grown somewhat thicker near or over Holy Head Island but still didn't seem to be a major threat. Darcy relayed Lowery's instructions about being tied to the pole to prevent them from being thrown about if the sea got rough.

"Does he think it will happen?"

"He said it is possible as the storms can come up quite suddenly. Pride of Pemberley is a strong ship, but she might find it difficult if the winds are extremely high."

"And you know how to tie the knot he mentioned?"

"Yes, though I have forgotten what it is called."

"No matter. When we see him next, *I* will ask him," she said, raising one eyebrow.

William just chuckled and shook his head. *That is my Elizabeth.*

A short while later as the Darcys read in Lowery's cabin, they heard a loud 'bloody hell' and a cry of, "Squall line. Man the sails."

A split second later, a hard wind slammed into the ship and threw William and Elizabeth to the deck.

Darcy crawled across the floor of the cabin, unable to take a breath but frantic about his wife. When he could finally breathe, he called out, "Elizabeth."

"Yes, I am well," came the weak response.

"Are you hurt?"

"Yes, but not seriously. Knocked the breath out of me."

"We need to reach the pole."

For the next few minutes, it took all the strength the two of them had to crawl over to and grasp the pole with both hands as the ship was tossed. Standing took even more effort, and the ship pitched due to the large waves created by the surging winds.

Darcy nearly had them tied to the post when the ship dropped out from under them and Darcy's head hit the pole and started bleeding. Elizabeth had her own injury from biting her lip.

"Hold onto the pole, Lizzy."

Elizabeth had to laugh as her husband never called her Lizzy, but Darcy had said it deliberately, in spite of preferring Elizabeth, in order to divert her from his bleeding forehead. He cautiously reached for his handkerchief and quickly dabbed at the blood flow until it stopped.

All this time, the ship was tossed up and down then to and fro as the winds kept slamming into her, and the waves would drop out from under her. They could hear the sailors on deck as orders were shouted and the men did what they could to stabilize the ship and keep her from being torn apart.

A loud ripping sound sent a spear of dread to Darcy's heart. One of the sails had surely been damaged.

"Hold tight, Elizabeth."

"Yes, my love."

As he heard the words, he felt his heart swell. He knew Elizabeth loved him, but this was the first time, she had used that particular expression. He kept his arms wrapped around her and the pole and kept her body pressed up against it.

Elizabeth screamed when without warning, the ship tilted sideways and seemed as if it would completely turn over. Darcy knew the rail on the lee side had to have gone completely underwater, and he was grateful when the ship righted itself. But he worried at the amount of water that flowed into the cabin under the door. *Please don't let the ship wreck and any of us drown.*

For the next hour, they gripped the pole and the ship bucked on the waves until they felt it couldn't take any more. When he heard a large crack, Darcy tensed. Without a doubt they had lost at least part of a mast. He could only hope it didn't land on the deck and kill anyone. The whole time the Darcys had been praying that all would get through the storm in one piece. The ship could be repaired. Lost lives could not.

The ship vibrated as the piece of mast landed on the deck with a loud thud. Tears were rolling down Elizabeth's cheeks as she worried about the men topside. They had been so kind to her and William, and she didn't want to see any of them harmed. *Please God, let everyone be well.*

Elizabeth was exhausted and wondering if it would ever end. She hung onto consciousness, so she wouldn't worry William. But he worried anyway at the slightly green tinge to his wife's face as the ship continued an up and down motion that was wreaking havoc with his own insides. He doubted she was doing any better.

The cries of the men on deck as they struggled to get the ship under control filtered through the howl of the storm. Abruptly, the wind slackened, the ship shuddered, and the men grew quiet. Then a cry of victory poured from the sailors. The squall had passed, and the ship was still intact. Lowery burst through the door of the cabin, fear etched into his features, obviously scared of what he would find.

"Are you both well?" He glanced between them.

Elizabeth just nodded as the men released her from the pole, and Darcy said he was worried about her. Once released, she cast up her accounts in the rubbish bin and promptly swooned.

"Elizabeth." Darcy was frantic. Picking her up, he gently placed her in the hammock wrapping her in a dry blanket. Her boots were soaked, and he stripped her feet bare and wrapped them with a dry towel planning to find her other boots and stockings.

"Elizabeth." Darcy continued to try to awaken his wife by talking to her and chafing her hands. In a few moments, he could see her eyelashes fluttering and felt his heart unclench. "Elizabeth, are you well?"

A small smile appeared, and she reassured him that she was not harmed. When apprised she had swooned, Elizabeth was indignant. "I have never swooned in my entire life."

"There is always a first time, my dear, and this was it."

Wanting to kiss her sweet lips, he refrained and silently lamented that he probably would not be able to for about a week until her lip healed. So, he was content to kiss her forehead…almost.

Lowery had left when Darcy started taking off Elizabeth's boots and stockings, but now he returned with news.

"Seems your lady ship has become a fortune hunter."

"The damage is that extensive?"

"We lost the spanker sails, the moonraker, and the skysail and the mast broke above the royal. Two of the big sails are ripped, and there is other minor damage as well."

"Captain Lowery, are all the men safe?"

He smiled. "Yes, thankfully, these men are a tough lot, though three have suffered broken bones, and all are bruised and battered from being tossed bout. Cook is working on them now. If infection doesn't develop, they should be well, Mrs. Darcy. Thank you for asking about them. They will be pleased."

"And I am thankful we have such a good crew. Thank the men for saving all of us and let them know there will be a bonus for all."

Lowery nodded his thanks for his men and left the cabin to see what he could do.

"Sweetheart, it looks like we may not make it to Liverpool this evening. Would you mind if we were a day or two late arriving at Pemberley?"

Taking his hand, she shook her head. "No, my darling, I would not mind. All are safe, and my prayers were answered. I am content."

He just nodded, closed his eyes, and laid his head along her side as he knelt on the floor by the hammock. A small delay would be of no consequence compared to what they had just been through.

Epilogue

It was two days before the ship limped into the Port of Liverpool and drew a large crowd. To the untrained eye, it looked as if Pride of Pemberley would not be salvageable. But Lowery knew better. It would cost a fair number of pounds, but the ship could be repaired and seaworthy with a bit of time. Until then, prospective buyers would be able to see and determine how tough the clipper ships were in weathering even a dangerous squall. In the meantime, the gawkers and the curious continued to pass by for the next few days with slack jaws and amazement that they had survived.

Darcy made arrangements for the crew's bonuses and invited Captain Lowery to have dinner with him and Elizabeth at their hotel just before they were to depart for Pemberley. This time, Elizabeth had desired to go straight to Pemberley without an overnight stop, and Darcy agreed. Arrangements were made for a carriage and outriders, and they left the next morning after sending an express to Georgiana that they would be arriving after dark.

***

Darkness had already fallen when they approached Lambton, and Darcy hired runners with torches to go before them for the five-mile trip to Pemberley. He was pleased that Mrs. Reynolds, the servants, his sister, and his cousin were all waiting on the steps as their carriage arrived with the jingling of harnesses and the crunching of gravel. He wasn't surprised that his sister ran to greet them with Richard following behind.

"Welcome, home. We have missed you both. How was your trip?"

"It was amazing, and we will tell you all about it when we have settled in on the morrow. In the meantime, may we descend from the coach?"

"Of course." And Georgiana was glad that it was dark as she felt her face grow warm.

As soon as Elizabeth's feet touched the ground, Georgiana gave her a big hug. "I am so glad you are home safely. I worried about you."

"And where is my hug, Georgie?"

William held her close for a moment and was thankful they were alive and home safe with family and friends.

"We have food ready for you both. Would you like to eat in the small dining room or in your bedchambers?"

"Would you mind the dining room, Elizabeth?"

"Not at all. We can visit with Georgiana and Richard before retiring."

"Why don't you refresh yourself while I care for the outriders and coachmen, and I will be with you in a quarter hour?"

Elizabeth smiled, nodded, and proceeded upstairs as Darcy went to his safe then paid the men who had gotten them safely home with nice bonuses for all. He breathed a sigh of relief. Elizabeth was safe, and he was the happiest man on earth. The loneliness he had experienced for years was gone, and he suspected that he would be a father in a few months. He couldn't wait.

***

To the surprise of everyone, both Darcys slept until noon. But when Georgiana and Richard heard of all that happened on their trip, especially concerning the ship, they understood why the couple was exhausted.

When they finally arrived for luncheon, Georgiana had to know all the details. Darcy demurred at first until Elizabeth commented. "Your sister has a right to know what happened to the blackguard, and that she need never worry about him again."

"What happened to him? I would prefer someone run him through."

"He wasn't run through, Richard, but he did die."

After hearing the details, Darcy was surprised that his sister shed a few tears over Wickham's death. But Richard was elated.

"Why tears, Georgiana? Do you still have a tendre for him?"

"No, brother. It's just that…he was a friend long ago, and now he is dead. 'Tis sad."

Richard scoffed and was going to make a scathing remark until Darcy shook his head at him, and he shut his mouth. Darcy understood how his sister felt.

All were quiet for the next few minutes, then Richard changed the subject and demanded more details of their trip. Between the two of them, the couple told them of the whole trip and extolled the entertainments of Patrick's pub. That they went incognito was entertaining to their sister and their cousin. Overall, they had a good trip, renewed old friendships, made new ones, and arrived home safely. They couldn't have asked for more.

But they were going to get more.

Two months after they arrived at Pemberley, Elizabeth confirmed that she was with child, and Darcy was overjoyed.

"You do realize that I knew you were *enceinte* from the beginning, do you not?"

"You could not have been aware. I was not aware."

"Ah, but my mother exhibited the same signs that you did, my love. The fatigue, the increased appetite, and the extreme emotions are how I knew. And I could not be happier to be a father. And the babe will have the loveliest, sweetest, most intelligent, and most wonderful mother in the world."

"It seems like his father is a most wonderful man also. I must say that I chose very well."

Darcy couldn't resist. In spite of the fact they were in the library, he took her in his arms and gave her a toe-curling kiss that made her nearly swoon. Mrs. Reynolds walked through the door, saw them, turned around, and walked right out the door again. The footmen swore that the stern housekeeper had a big smile on her face as she went down the hallway toward the kitchen with a spring in her step. *My boy is happy. I couldn't be more pleased. They both chose well.*

Excerpt from 'Darcy vs Bingley'

Foreshadow of Things to Come

"Sweetheart, I'm only going to stay for a few minutes, but I wanted to apprise you that my solicitor is drawing up the settlement papers. If I am moving too quickly, please let me know, but I would like to ask your father's blessing as soon as possible. Bingley mentioned that he is quite in love with your eldest sister and wishes to be able to announce his engagement at his ball."

"Oho, Mr. Darcy. You would ask for my father's blessing even before asking me? Tsk, tsk."

And he couldn't resist those kissable lips and proceeded to brush his lightly over hers until she gently grabbed his face and let him know how she felt.

"I cannot stay, Elizabeth. I would hate for your father to reproach me for not adhering to propriety any more than I have." Getting on one knee, he took her hand in his and asked, "Will you make me the happiest man on earth by becoming my wife, Miss Elizabeth?"

"My family—and yours, I daresay—will proclaim that we are candidates for Bedlam, but my answer is yes. I feel as if I have known you forever, and I don't believe I could live without you."

As he pulled her to her feet to give her another toe-curling kiss, the skies opened up pouring rainwater down the front of her dress and the back of his neck despite his cravat. A cloudburst on the scale of the Noachian flood struck both and soaked them within seconds. "Come. We need to get you back to Longbourn."

"Oh, but not the way we came up. I got caught like this before and slipped as I was descending. There are too many rocks this direction, and I had bruises for three weeks. This way is more of a gentle incline, and if we lose our footing, it is much better for going down. Just mud." Laughing aloud, she led him to the side of where they had been sitting and through a narrow place in the rocks. "It should be an easy descent if we can stay on our feet."

"Oh, doubting one. I am very sure on my feet. Take my hand, and I'll get us down."

"Oh, no, Mr. Darcy. The footing can be treacherous here, and it would be best if we make our way down separately."

"I bow to your experience, and I will let you be my guide."

As Elizabeth started down the slight incline, she could feel her boots start sliding. "Beware, William, it is getting slick rapidly." She had barely said the words when her feet slipped, and she went down the side of Oakham Mount with a shriek.

"Elizabeth!" Darcy panicked then he went down as well.

Chapter I

Fitzwilliam Darcy had traveled from London that day and was informed on his arrival that Charles Bingley expected him to attend the assembly in Meryton that evening. Having spent the last few days in completing all his affairs before coming to Netherfield Park in Hertfordshire, Darcy had planned on relaxing for the rest of the day and retiring early as he was rather fatigued. Instead, he indulged his friend and attended the assembly where he was introduced to a family with five daughters.

Wincing at the comments as he, Bingley, Bingley's two sisters, and his brother-in-law arrived, Darcy expected to despise the evening. In fact, he even made a disparaging remark— about no one being tolerable enough in looks to tempt him to dance—that he regretted the moment he made it. But he was surprised to find that the congenial atmosphere and especially the 'fine eyes' of the second eldest Bennet daughter caught his attention, enough so that he *did* ask her to dance. Bingley's raised eyebrows indicated his shock that his friend readily joined the country dance with Miss Elizabeth Bennet when he usually had to be coerced into doing so.

Caroline Bingley, Charles' younger unwed sister, glared at the couple as they went through the moves of the lively dance. Unknown to Bingley or Mr. Darcy, Miss Bingley was determined to wed Darcy by hook or crook. Compromising him did not deter her one bit. When she saw the smile on his face as he danced with Elizabeth, she was determined that a compromise it would be, and she planned it for the middle of the night.

"Thank you, Mr. Darcy. I enjoyed having you as my partner." Elizabeth smiled and blushed as Darcy kissed her hand.

"Miss Elizabeth, it was all my pleasure. Ordinarily, I don't enjoy dancing with someone with whom I'm unacquainted.

However, this evening I'm delighted to have had this dance with you and wondered if I might have the last one as well."

Elizabeth paused. Her first impression of Darcy when he and his friends arrived had been that he disdained being there and was haughty and proud. However, she had discovered on accepting his request to dance with her that he was not only extremely handsome, he was charming, intelligent and had a most engaging smile. For him to ask for a second dance left her speechless, but not for long.

"I would like that very much, Mr. Darcy." She curtseyed, and he bowed, and then he accompanied her back to her sister, Jane.

***

As the two young women watched Darcy head toward the other side of the ballroom, Jane inquired, "Lizzy, what did you do to attract Mr. Darcy?"

"I don't know, Jane, but I'm not displeased. He's not like anyone I've met before."

"And you like him, don't you?"

"Yes, I find I do like him very much. He's also asked for the last dance."

Jane reached over with a smile and squeezed her sister's hand. She also liked the time she spent with Mr. Bingley finding him very amiable and likable. Being the eldest child in her family, she wanted the best for her siblings as well. *I wonder if Mr. Darcy will be the one for Lizzy? I've never seen her as interested in a young man as she seems to be with him.*

Glancing at Lizzy, Jane watched as her sister gazed around the room then suddenly blushed and looked down. When Jane followed the direction of her sister's look, she spotted Mr. Darcy smiling at Elizabeth, and a knowing smile curved Jane's lips also.

Caroline Bingley, however, scowled as she noticed the object of Darcy's interest. *Definitely, I need to compromise him tonight before that country chit gets her hooks into him. That will not happen!*

***

As the music for the last dance ended, Darcy took Elizabeth's hand and led her from the dance floor. He was delighted to note that her face was flushed from the exertion, and with her gentle smile, it made her look almost beautiful.

On impulse, he asked, "May I call on you on the morrow?"

Taken by surprise, Elizabeth's eyes widened at first then sparkled as she contemplated the handsome man coming to see her. "Yes, you may, Mr. Darcy. I look forward to your visit."

He smiled as she turned a pretty shade of pink. Then taking her hand, he brushed his lips across the back of it as her blush deepened. "The morrow cannot come too soon, Miss Elizabeth."

Darcy was pleased as he walked away. If he continued to find pleasure in her company, he would consider asking for a courtship. After all, her hand had trembled when he kissed it. *I wonder if she is as attracted to me as I am to her? Perhaps, I can find out when I call on her.*

***

Jane and Elizabeth were quiet on the way back to Longbourn, but their mother filled the silence and didn't seem to notice they weren't talking much as she exclaimed how pleased she was that both young women had danced twice with the men from Netherfield.

"Just think, girls, Mr. Bingley and Mr. Darcy are such eligible young men. Mr. Bingley has five thousand pounds, and Mr. Darcy has ten thousand pounds per annum. Lady Lucas told me so. Oh, the carriages and the pin money you both will have. I couldn't ask for more for my daughters. We won't starve in the hedgerows after your father dies."

"Mama, don't even say that. Papa is very healthy and should live for many more years. Jane and I don't have to marry this instant or any time soon."

"Lizzy, you set your cap for Mr. Darcy. A man in his position and with his wealth will never take you seriously if you don't. Jane, you too, need to be very amiable toward Mr. Bingley. He had his eye on you all evening. I think he would have danced more than two with you if propriety would have allowed it."

"Oh, Mama," Jane exclaimed in embarrassment.

"Mama, Mr. Darcy and Mr. Bingley said they would call on the morrow. Please give Jane and me time to get acquainted with them before you push us to the altar. She and I both would like to have love matches and not marry for wealth alone."

"You listen to me, Lizzy. You might want a love match, but money is important as well. It's just as easy to fall in love with a rich man as with a poor man. You, mark my words."

All this time, Kitty and Lydia were giggling and whispering about the militia that would soon return from maneuvers that had prevented the men from attending the assembly. They were also amused by their mother's comments to their older sisters. Mary just shook her head at her younger siblings for their silly and hoydenish ways. Nobody noticed when she rolled her eyes at them as well.

Arriving at Longbourn, the young women disembarked the coach and headed upstairs after giving their outer garments to Mr. Hill. Nobody wanted to listen to Mrs. Bennet rant about them marrying and saving everyone from starving in the hedgerows. And they were exhausted after a lively evening at the assembly.

Jane and Lizzy stayed up for a while and discussed the merits of the two men from Netherfield. And when they finally slept, both dreamed pleasant dreams of the morrow.

***

Darcy was pleased. Instead of experiencing a horrible evening with those beneath him, he'd found the company more than tolerable, especially Miss Elizabeth. He was dazzled by the twinkle in her eye as she teased him, and she had made him laugh for the first time in a long while even since before Ramsgate and the devastating event of his sister's near elopement with George Wickham. The dastard had convinced her she was in love with him. His poor sister had still not recovered from Wickham's declaration that he was only after her thirty thousand pound dowry.

Then he smiled when he thought of Miss Elizabeth. Her liveliness was such that if they did marry, she would be good for Georgiana and he might get his sister back.

Exhausted from his travels that day and the assembly that night, Darcy stripped and fell into bed and immediately succumbed to sleep unaware that he would have an early morning visitor.

***

Caroline Bingley quietly tip-toed down the corridor to the guest wing and soon arrived at Darcy's door. Turning the knob that she had oiled earlier, she silently moved to the opposite side of the bed from where she surmised Darcy slept. Stripping off her nightgown, she slid under the covers and touched Darcy's bare back.

For a moment, nothing happened except for Darcy's continued light snores. Then they stopped, and he catapulted out of the bed. "Who's there?" Half asleep, he staggered toward the chair with his banyan knowing he was as naked as the day he was born. In the process, he banged his knee on the chair which made him swear profusely as he covered himself.

"Mr. Darcy. Come back to bed," Caroline crooned.

"Miss Bingley?"

"Mr. Darcy. Can I help with anything?" Darcy's valet came out of the dressing room where his cot was placed. The light of his candle illuminated part of the room, and when Caroline saw him, she screamed.

Bingley—who couldn't sleep—was heading down to his study for a nightcap when he heard his sister's scream. Running to Darcy's door, he threw it open and demanded to know what was going on.

"I believe, Bingley, that Caroline has tried to compromise me." Turning to Higgins, he said, "I don't want one word mentioned about this, do you understand?"

"Mr. Darcy, I never saw a thing."

"Good man. I knew I could rely on you."

"Caroline, what's the meaning of this." Bingley's eyes grew wide. Shocked, he demanded, "Are you naked?"

His sister pulled the sheet up higher, a fiery red blush rising into her cheeks.

By this time, Darcy's fury had risen to the point that he would put a stop to Caroline's machinations forever. Glaring at her until she dropped her eyes, he moved until his knees touched the bed. He remained silent until he felt like he could refrain from throttling her if she said anything. Then he opened his mouth.

"Miss Bingley. Is it your desire to marry me?"

"Oh, yes, Fitzwilliam. I have long wanted to marry you and become mistress of Pemberley."

"Why?" Darcy ignored her using his Christian name, but only for the moment.

"I love you, of course."

Darcy laughed and continued to laugh until Caroline got the point he thought she was ridiculous.

"If you truly did, I would handle this differently. But since the only things you love are my money, my status, my home, and yourself, I will say what will happen to you if we did marry."

"Oh, Mr. Darcy, I know you would make me an excellent husband."

"You think that, do you?"

"Oh, yes." Smiling and fluttering her eyelashes at him, she tried to make the best of a situation that was rapidly going awry.

Darcy stood quietly for a moment with his eyes narrowed and his arms folded across his chest. "Well, let me apprise you of how it would actually be should we marry. First of all, there would only be a small wedding before a parson with a special license. I have no interest in bragging about marrying you."

Bingley's sister gasped at the sarcastic note in Darcy's voice.

"Second, I will own you, and you would stay at Pemberley. No trips to London, no seasons, no fancy dresses or anything connected with the *ton.* If I have business in London, I will go alone."

"Now, Darcy…"

"Silence, Bingley!"

And Bingley shut up. In a moment, he began to realize what Darcy was doing.

"Third, your dowry of thirty thousand pounds will go into Pemberley's account for the benefit of the estate and the tenants and servants connected with it. You'll not see another farthing of it."

Caroline was livid and yelled at him, "You can't do that."

"Oh, yes, I can. I will be your husband, and I *will tell you* what you may do."

By this time, tears began to flow down Caroline's cheeks, and she was beginning to understand that what she started, Darcy was going to finish.

"Fourth, you will receive only one hundred pounds pin money."

"A quarter?" Miss Bingley asked.

"Per annum."

Caroline's mouth dropped open as she just stared at him.

"Fifth, you will not be allowed to make any changes at Pemberley. The running of Pemberley is set in stone as far as you are concerned. Mrs. Reynolds does a marvelous job of handling the affairs of my house. You will not be allowed to redecorate, change the furniture or anything in my house except for your own quarters, which I will never enter. And you will not be allowed in my rooms either."

"But, Fitzwilliam…"

Darcy leaned forward and roared in her face, "I did not give you permission to use my Christian name, Miss Bingley."

Even though she quailed at his shout, Caroline stiffened her spine. "But you will need an heir for Pemberley."

"But I don't need you or a male heir," Darcy spat. "Pemberley is not entailed, and I will leave everything to Georgiana should anything happen to me. Should the worst happen, you will have to move back with Bingley or the Hursts."

"But, but…"

"No buts. Sixth, if you ever create a problem for Georgiana, I will file for divorce. I will survive it, but I'm not sure your reputation will."

"Divorce? You would divorce me?" she squeaked.

"In a heartbeat." Darcy's scowl left nothing to Caroline's imagination. She knew he meant it.

Bingley just stood on the sideline and tried not to smile. He had a small twinge of conscience, but he knew his sister deserved this. For several years, Darcy had been his best friend and treated the Bingley family well. For his sister to do his friend this way was abominable. So, he appreciated what Darcy was saying.

"Lastly, married or not, if you ever mention any of this to your sister or her husband or anyone else, I will be apprised of it. My aunt, Lady Matlock, knows everything that goes on in London. She *will* find out, and she will apprise me as well. And I will inform all the *ton* of everything you did this night, every single detail."

Caroline blanched at this as she knew details of this night's debacle would definitely ruin her as far as society was concerned. She also knew she had lost the battle as well as the war for mistress of Pemberley. It would never be no matter what she did.

"So, if you insist on marrying me, I will make your life miserable."

"No," she said with a sigh. "No, I will not insist, and Charles will not either. I didn't realize you disliked me so much."

Softening his tone, Darcy said, "I didn't intend to dislike you, Miss Bingley. But I do dislike your cattiness and disdain for others. I do hate your selfish attitude and your bullying of Charles and your sister. And I despise the fact that you will act in an unloving manner to get what you want no matter how badly you have to behave or whom you have to hurt. I had known you not even a month before I realized that you were the last person on earth I would ever marry."

Bingley and Darcy both hoped when all was said and done that Caroline would learn a powerful lesson and become a better person. Only time would tell.

Pulling herself together, Miss Bingley asked that the men give her some privacy so she could dress and return to her bedchamber. And they complied.

After she left, Bingley turned to his friend. "Darcy, you did what you had to do. I hope my sister takes this to heart."

Darcy just nodded then closed and locked the door when Bingley left the room. Going to the dressing room, he started to thank Higgins when the man instead said, "Do you wish for me to sleep in front of the servants' door in case she comes back?"

"Perhaps, that would be best." Darcy sighed. He was not a cruel man, and he wished this night hadn't been necessary. However, Bingley's sibling had surprised him, and he wouldn't allow that to happen again.

The more he thought about Elizabeth Bennet, the more he wanted to know about her, and he could picture her at Pemberley as well.

Darcy took off his banyan and crawled wearily under the covers wearing nothing but a smile and had the most pleasant dreams he could ever remember about a pretty lady and her very fine eyes.

Chapter II

The next morning, Darcy awoke with a smile on his face. Stretching on the bed, he realized he had had the most refreshing sleep in a while and grinned when he remembered his pleasant dreams about a certain lovely young lady. For a few minutes, he lay still and thought about the visit to the Bennet's home later in the morning. What should he do or what would he say to Miss Elizabeth? *Do I really desire a courtship with her? If so, how soon should I request it? And where?*

However, his thoughts went from joy to his confrontation with Miss Bingley a few hours earlier. As he pondered on what had transpired, his head began to hurt. The more he recalled, the angrier he became and the more his head ached until he seriously debated about not breaking his fast with Bingley's family. *But I dare not abstain. Miss Bingley needs to understand that Bingley and I will not tolerate any more of her questionable conduct. I must attend breakfast with the others.* And he grimaced at the thought.

"Higgins."

"Yes, Mr. Darcy?"

"I'm experiencing a headache. Do you still have some of your powders with you?"

"Yes, sir. Give me a moment to retrieve them from my luggage."

A half hour later, fortified with the headache powder, shaved, and dressed, Darcy was ready to face the day and Miss Bingley.

***

"Good morning, Darcy. I hope you slept well."

"Good morning, Bingley, Hurst, Mrs. Hurst…Miss Bingley." Caroline flushed as she noted Darcy's slight hesitation in acknowledging her. "I slept as well as could be expected."

Bingley nodded in agreement and refrained from laughing out loud.

As his headache had abated somewhat, Darcy realized that he was quite hungry and appreciated the abundance and variety of food on the sideboard. Filling his plate with bacon, ham, kippers, eggs, and toast, he seated himself beside Hurst although it put him across the table from Caroline. However, it was much better than having to sit right next to her. To be close enough to touch her would tempt him beyond restraint as he wished to give her a good shaking for her actions during the night. However, he was too much of a gentleman to succumb to such temptation. Or was he? Even Darcy had no answer for that.

"Caroline, did you get up in the night? I thought I heard your door slam in the early hours this morning."

Miss Bingley blushed as she turned to her sister. "Yes, I did. I couldn't sleep so I thought perhaps walking a bit would make me sleepy. But I didn't walk long as I was very tired."

Since her sister had done this before, Louisa just nodded in understanding. What did surprise her was what Caroline said next.

"Charles, the assembly last night was so dreadfully boring, I've decided to return to London and my friends."

Darcy had to suppress a grin when he heard her decision. The quicker she departed, the better he would feel about the whole affair.

"But, Caroline. You are my hostess. How will I manage without you?"

"Caroline, you cannot possibly leave this soon," Louisa chimed in. "Gilbert and I came to relax, not for me to wait on Charles." Bingley promptly frowned at this comment and opened his mouth to say something but was interrupted by Hurst with his mouth half full.

"I quite agree that you should stay, Caroline. Louisa is tired from hosting at our home over the last three months. And with the baby due in four months, she has earned a rest." With that, he nearly choked on his food until he had finished swallowing it and washing it down with a big swig of his coffee.

Darcy just rolled his eyes and kept his head down as he continued to eat his breakfast and the debate continued. Since his friend was so amiable and even tempered, Darcy was surprised when an exasperated Bingley addressed his sibling.

"Caroline, you cannot leave. I won't let you. I plan to host a ball in three weeks, and I need you to be my hostess until then and for the ball itself. You are knowledgeable about the decorations and the food to be served. After that, if you wish to leave, I will not stop you.

"But, Charles..."

"But, Charles, nothing, Caroline. I have increased your dowry to thirty thousand pounds. I have tolerated your outrageous bills for your many gowns, most of which I don't remember ever seeing you wear, and I've said nothing about your scathing comments about anything and everybody you disdain. All I have asked in return is that you be my hostess until you or I marry. I do not believe I am being excessive in that expectation."

It was all Darcy could do to not burst out in laughter at Charles' words. If he dared, he would clap his hands and yell 'Bravo' as his best friend stood his ground with his sister. As it was, all he *could* do was bite his tongue and refrain from taking another morsel of food until his internal amusement abated.

In the meantime, a subdued Caroline agreed to stay, and with a sigh, she continued her meal until she finished and excused herself.

"I wonder what the matter is with Caroline, Gilbert. She doesn't seem herself this morning."

"Maybe, she has dyspepsia, my dear. Being around such country bumpkins may have put her off her food."

"Perhaps." But Louisa didn't believe it for a minute. Something was bothering her sister, and she *would* find out what the problem was.

Darcy became alarmed when he noted the doubt in Mrs. Hurst's voice. Aware that the two sisters were thicker than thieves, he knew Caroline would be bound to tell Louisa what happened in the night in spite of his threat. *What shall I do if she does tell Mrs.*

Hurst? I really don't want to ruin her for Charles' sake. I must think this through and speak with Charles as well.

By this time, Louisa had finished her meal and excused herself to follow Caroline upstairs.

Hoping that Hurst would take a nap instead of joining them, Darcy asked Charles if he wished to ride to Longbourn and pay a call on the Bennets.

Charles' face lit up with the delight he so frequently displayed. "You will not leave without me, Darcy. Oh, to see the lovely Miss Bennet again. She is definitely an angel."

Darcy rolled his eyes and replied, "Every pretty young woman is an angel to you, Charles. And on how many occasions have you fallen in love?"

His friend flushed in embarrassment as he acknowledged that Darcy was correct. "But, this time I think it is different. Miss Bennet is like no other young woman I've met to date. There is something about her that calls to my heart. Perhaps, she is the one I should marry."

With Charles' pronouncement, Darcy's alarm grew. After hearing Mrs. Bennet's enthusiastic comments concerning his and Bingley's annual incomes, the night before, and how his friend seemed enamored with her eldest daughter, he was afraid the younger man would find himself in an unequal marriage, a fate he would not wish on his worst enemy.

"Charles, I care for you and your welfare. I have no other friend that's as close to me as you other than my cousin Richard. Please, take time to make sure that she returns your regard. When the time comes, I want you to have a splendid marriage, full of joy and love. After all, you just met her last night. Promise me you will not make any hasty decisions and will go slowly getting to know Miss Bennet."

Bingley nodded. "I know you're right, and I promise I will not rush in making her acquaintance. But, know this, if she shares my regard, I *will* ask her to marry me."

"And that's as it should be. If that happens, I will wish you both happy."

With that, Bingley finished eating and with a big smile hurried upstairs to change into his riding clothes.

Mr. Hurst just sat for a minute and looked at Darcy until the object of his gaze shifted uncomfortably.

"Hurst, you have a question?"

"No, no question. Just a 'thank you' for your words to Charles. I like my brother and have learned to love my wife. However, I am under no delusions that Charles can be a little naïve as well as a little childlike in some of his behavior. I too wish him happy when he finds the right lady to woo and wed. Whether it is Miss Bennet or someone else matters not. I would see Charles content in his marriage. 'Til now, he has been a little precipitous in thinking he's found an angel. Yet, he does seem to be a little more thoughtful in regard to Miss Bennet. I hope he will follow your excellent suggestion."

Darcy's face heated with Hurst's praise, and he just quietly said, "I will do my best to encourage him to be reasonable."

"Have a good ride and a nice visit with the Bennet ladies…including Miss Elizabeth." Hurst's smirk let Darcy know the man had noted his attentions to Elizabeth the night before, and his face grew warmer still.

I wonder how many others saw how smitten I was with the lady with the lovely eyes. Should I care? I must as I owe my family a duty to marry well. With a grimace, he shoved his thoughts aside and looked forward to seeing a lively lady and making her a friend or maybe more.

***

In a quarter hour, Bingley was downstairs, and the two men headed toward Netherfield's stables. Shortly thereafter, they rode around the Park's property until time to call on the Bennets.

As Darcy and Bingley considered Netherfield's grounds, Darcy voiced his concern for the happenings of the night before.

"Bingley, I worry that Caroline will tell Louisa what transpired last night. I have no desire to ruin her by divulging what occurred, but I do need to ensure that it does not come to the ears of the *ton* as the gossips will destroy her reputation and her prospects of making a good match. Your sister is not very likable—I daresay— but she should have the opportunity to marry and raise a family."

Bingley sighed. "My sincerest apologies for the actions of my sister, Darcy. If I had any idea she was considering a compromise…"

"I know, and I don't blame you. My worry is, how do I proceed from here? And will it affect my interest in Miss Elizabeth?"

"Miss Elizabeth? Darcy, do not tell me. You are smitten by the lovely Miss Elizabeth?" Bingley chortled in glee as he recalled the evening. "But, of course you are. You danced with her twice last night and with no others except my sisters. You have never done that before. Darcy's in love." And with that, Charles whooped with laughter as Darcy's face grew warm.

"Darcy, you're even blushing." That observation brought even more laughter as Bingley's friend's face turned a bright red.

"Desist, Bingley. I'm in no mood for your teasing this morning. My headache is returning."

"My apologies again, Darcy. You need to be your best when you visit Miss Elizabeth. Although not as comely as my angel, she is very pretty, and she has very nice eyes as well." At Darcy's expression, Bingley actually snickered at his friend while Darcy just rolled his eyes.

"Bingley…" Darcy threatened.

"All is well, my friend. I couldn't resist. Fitzwilliam Darcy is finally enamored of a young lady after avoiding the machinations of hundreds of willing members of the *ton* for years." Darcy glared as Charles doubled over in laughter ignoring his friend's protest.

"I acknowledge that some have pursued me in spite of my disinterest but not hundreds. How could I ever offer for a woman who only wants my status, my money, and my home? When I marry, it will be a love match, and I'm willing to wait."

"And if Miss Elizabeth is the one?"

"If she proves to be the one, I will pursue a proper courtship." Darcy sighed, and they rode for a while as each contemplated the Bennet sisters.

Finally, Darcy said, "I do worry somewhat about the Bennets. Mrs. Bennet seemed rather vulgar and uncouth. She could be heard above the crowd as she discussed our incomes with no restraint. She was particularly delighted that you danced with Miss Bennet twice also and spoke as if you were already betrothed."

"Well…I suppose that my eagerness to dance with Miss Bennet a second time could cause some speculation. Although I came here to consider purchasing Netherfield Park, I don't think I would mind finding the lady of my dreams as well." It was now Bingley's turn to blush as he seriously considered pursuing the lovely blond woman with sparkling blue eyes.

"And how many times have you been sure that you had found the lady of your dreams? How many times have you fallen in love?" Darcy reminded him again.

Bingley's protest was subdued at first but strengthened as he spoke. "Too many, Darcy, I admit…But this time it's different. Miss Bennet isn't like the others. She's…She's genuine. I love her smile and her quiet and mild spirit. It appeals to me as no other personality has in the past. She could be the one I marry and be happy with." Charles' blush intensified as he thought of waking up to the lovely Miss Bennet every morning. *No, she would be Mrs. Jane Bingley.* And he smiled in contemplation.

For the rest of the time until they would head toward Longbourn, the two men looked over the property Bingley was considering. Netherfield Park was the second largest in Hertfordshire with the largest being the Bennets' property, Longbourn Village. Bingley looked forward to learning how to run a large estate from the man who owned the most land in the county of Derbyshire. George Darcy had been wise in training his son to take charge of

Pemberley and all that it encompassed. And Darcy had done well, increasing his wealth from that of his father, and in caring for the many tenants and servants who helped with the estate. Bingley appreciated his good fortune in knowing such a man and calling him 'friend.'

Chapter III

Louisa entered Caroline's room without knocking, which was usual for the sisters. For years before her marriage to Hurst, Caroline's sibling treated both their bedchambers the same. The informality had never been a problem until today.

"Go away, Louisa. I don't want to chat right now."

Louisa's eyebrows rose into her hairline. Never had her sister missed an opportunity to gossip. And Louisa wanted to discuss the assembly the night before and how humiliating the country bumpkins had been.

"Caroline, what's the matter with you. You're not yourself this morning. Did that atrocious assembly upset you?"

"No...yes...no." And Caroline just kept pacing the floor looking miserable all the while.

After years of her sibling's company, Louisa knew that something was definitely amiss. She wouldn't leave until Caroline told her what had upset her since last night. *She'd been fine when we arrived home from that insipid country dance, so it has to be something that happened afterward.*

Caroline was halted in place by her sister's hands on her shoulders. "Caroline, please tell me what is wrong."

"I can't."

"You can't or won't?"

Caroline sighed. "Both."

Determined more than ever to discover the problem, Louisa urged her to sit down.

Since Caroline was always a model of grace and decorum, her sister's mouth dropped open when she simply flopped in the chair in front of the fireplace. Alarm for her sister and closest friend increased as Louisa had never seen Caroline sad. Even when their parents died, her sibling refused to appear distraught. She was sad at the loss but would not allow that to be seen by others. She had always kept a stiff upper lip in all situations. But now, she had tears starting to course down her cheeks, and Louisa's alarm grew.

"Caro, I have never seen you cry before. Please confide in me."

"I can't."

"Why not?"

"There will be nasty repercussions if I do."

"Why?"

"Please, leave me alone, Louisa. Go away."

Louisa knelt down beside her sister and gathered her in her arms. This was too much for Caroline, who began crying harder and with great sobs. After a time, her tears slowed and finally stopped as she hiccupped twice.

"Here's my handkerchief."

"Thank you."

Louisa just sat and looked at her as she contemplated how to worm the information out of her sister. "Feeling better?"

"Yes, thank you."

That was the straw that broke the camel's back. Her sister was never that polite except in public, certainly never with family. Louisa was more determined than ever to find out what had disturbed her sister to that extent.

Getting up and pulling the other chair close to Caroline, Louisa sat, took her hand, looked her in the eye, and softly said, "I promise I will say nothing to anyone. Please tell me what is wrong."

Louisa was not only Caroline's sister and closest friend, she was also the one with whom she shared any and all gossip. She just couldn't remain silent. After a few more tears, she began telling her sister of her attempted compromise of Mr. Darcy.

"I was mortified with three men in the room, and I was as naked as the day I was born under that sheet. And I'm sure they knew as well."

"But what happened? Did Mr. Darcy throw you out?"

"Not at first. He proceeded to tell me how he would make my life miserable."

"Mr. Darcy? I never would have thought he had a cruel streak."

"Nor would I. I supposed he would eventually accept the compromise, and I would become mistress of Pemberley. Oh, how I longed for that position as his wife." And her tears began again.

"Caroline, are you in love with Mr. Darcy?" Louisa did love her husband and knew if Caro loved Mr. Darcy, it would be heartbreaking for her.

"Good heavens no. Love didn't enter into it at all. I deserve to be his wife and mistress of Pemberley. After all, I've waited four years for the man to recognize I am the best lady for that position."

By this time, Louisa was curious about what else Darcy had told Caroline, and she began pressing for more information.

"He said if he married me it would be a tiny wedding with no fanfare. He also said he would only give me one hundred pounds per annum pin money." She stopped for a moment as she thought about what else he had said. As she remembered, she grew angry. "And he threatened to divorce me if I ever hurt Georgiana. As if I would hurt that sweet girl."

Louisa looked away from her sister and grimaced. She knew Caro was more than capable of hurting and even ruining anyone she decided upon. She had already done that with two rivals for a suitor's affection when she first came out, although the man had left her for another with a larger dowry anyway.

Turning back, Louisa asked, "Did he say anything else?"

"He stated he would make my life miserable. He would leave me at Pemberley and never take me back to London for the season."

For her part, Louisa kept pushing her sister as she knew there was more. "Is that all he said?"

"No. The worst of it was that all my dowry would be used for the estate and the tenants. He said I would see nothing of it ever again."

"But, Caroline, if you married, your dowry would be his."

"No, no, no. When I marry, I'll have it stipulated that my dowry stays mine."

"But, Caroline…"

Caroline started to reply when she remembered what else Darcy had declared, and her eyes opened wide.

"What is it?"

Covering her mouth with her hand, in horror she said, "Mr. Darcy said if I told anyone about what happened, even you, he would ruin me with the *ton*. Louisa, you must never even breathe a word about what happened, even to Gilbert."

"Caro, Mr. Darcy is an honorable man. I cannot see him deliberately ruining someone, not even you. He could not be that spiteful."

"Well, he said it, and he has two witnesses who can attest to it: his valet and Charles."

"Didn't Charles object to what Mr. Darcy declared?"

"No, he did not. I expected him to defend me, but he didn't. He agreed with Mr. Darcy." Outrage colored Caroline's voice as her hands clenched on the arms of the chair.

"Shhh. Keep your voice down. You don't want the servants learning about this. Nor do you want Mr. Darcy to find out you spoke to me."

Caroline shuddered. "No, he mustn't find out. Oh, what am I to do?"

"Caro, you are my sister. I love you. We must figure out how to get you in Mr. Darcy's good graces again. Now, this is what we'll do."

For the next two hours, the sisters discussed how to appease the great man and for Caroline to keep her dignity.

Chapter IV

Darcy checked his pocket watch and returned it to his waistcoat pocket as the two men determined that it was time to call at Longbourn. The assembly had ended late the night before, and they assumed that most of the Bennet ladies would still be abed. Why they felt that the two eldest might be awake was mostly wishful thinking on their part. And, in case they had erred on the time, they would be gracious to the entire family if need be.

"Gentlemen, if I may have your names, I will inquire if the family is at home."

The two visitors were a little astonished that Mr. Hill was attired and just as aloof as any butler of the *ton*. It seemed that they might have miscalculated the Bennets' place in Meryton society. They had no idea that Mrs. Bennet entertained four and twenty families in the area and was known for setting a magnificent table much to the chagrin of Mr. Bennet's purse.

Taking the men's cards, Hill left them at the door to inquire if Mr. Bennet was at home. Returning in short order, he informed them that Mr. Bennet would see them in his library.

All the while, the owner of Longbourn contemplated the possibility of entertainment from Mr. Darcy and Mr. Bingley. He had no illusions that they had come to visit him. With five lovely daughters, there was no doubt as to why they had called.

Bennet arose as the two men came through the door. "Mr. Bingley, Mr. Darcy. I see you are out early this fine morning. How may I help you?"

Both Darcy and Bingley were a little chagrined at not being shown to a parlor where the ladies might be. Instead, each was beginning to worry they might not even see their ladies at all. Why did Mr. Bennet have them shown to his sanctuary instead?

"Have a seat, gentlemen. May I offer you some tea? Or would you prefer coffee?"

Although Bingley enjoyed both coffee and tea, Darcy's preferred drink of choice was coffee.

After ringing for Mrs. Hill and ordering coffee for all three, Bennet leaned back, folded his hands in his lap, and smiled as he contemplated the fun to come. "Did you enjoy the assembly last night? It was certainly a lively one, perhaps more so than you might experience at a ball in Town. We country folk enjoy getting together and having a rousing good evening."

Bingley grinned and agreed. "It was a marvelous time. So many beautiful young ladies, and the dancing was wonderful. I don't know when I've enjoyed an evening more."

"And you, Mr. Darcy. Did you enjoy the evening?"

"I did, though I daresay I would have enjoyed it more if I hadn't been a little fatigued after traveling from London earlier in the day."

"Ah, but you were not so fatigued as to avoid dancing twice with my Lizzy. What are you about, Mr. Darcy?"

The slight frown on the man's face was beginning to unnerve Darcy a little. He was beginning to feel like a mouse within the paws of a very playful cat.

Mr. Bennet could see that the distinguished visitor had shown a preference to his favorite daughter, and he wasn't sure how he felt about that. He knew that one day he would lose her when she married; he just didn't wish it to be soon.

Darcy squirmed in his chair and heartily wanted to loosen his cravat but was hesitant to let Elizabeth's father know how uncomfortable he was with this interrogation. The only thing he knew to do was to be honest, and so he was.

"Miss Elizabeth is a lovely young woman. I appreciated her wit and intelligence and…and would enjoy the opportunity to know her better." This time, Darcy couldn't avoid loosening his cravat a little while Bennet laughed internally over the man's discomfort.

"Yes, she is. And…she is my favorite daughter." He held up a hand to forestall any protest Mr. Darcy might have. "I know I ought not to have favorites as I love all my daughters, but Lizzy and I are close. She is my chess opponent and beats me at my own game at least half of the time. She is also the most widely read of anyone in my family, and we debate the merits of the classics frequently. I'm proud of the fact that she reads several languages and keeps up reading the newspapers even following the war with Boney. She can hold her own on many different topics." Mr. Bennet leveled a warning gaze on Darcy. "However, most men don't appreciate her intelligence, and some have even labeled her a bluestocking on occasion."

At a soft tapping on the door, Mr. Bennet's comments stopped. "Come."

Mrs. Hill entered with a tray containing a coffeepot, three cups with saucers, a jug of milk, sugar, and assorted biscuits. And for a few moments, the three men were occupied with getting a cup prepared as they liked their coffee and acquiring a few biscuits.

Mr. Bennet waited until Darcy took a bite of one of the biscuits and then asked, "What say you, Mr. Darcy? What interest do you have in my second eldest daughter?"

Darcy nearly choked on the biscuit and spent no little time chewing and swallowing then washing it down with a sip of coffee. Clearing his throat, he croaked then cleared it again and spoke. "Mr. Bennet, I assure you my intentions are honorable. I admit I'm attracted to Miss Elizabeth as I've never been attracted before. She…She is refreshingly different. I would like to know her better with a possible courtship and proposal in mind.

To this point, Bingley and Bennet both had suppressed smiles at his friend's discomposure. And Bennet sighed internally as he had known that this day would eventually arrive, but he would not avoid his responsibility as a father. He needed to know more about Mr. Darcy. His Lizzy would not marry just anybody. She needed someone who would love and cherish and protect her as she deserved. And he understood that there were few men who would meet his exacting standards for a husband. There were also few men who would take a wife such as his favorite and let her be herself. Most would want to mold her into a biddable wife, and that would kill Elizabeth's spirit. Bennet would not allow it.

"And, you sir, what would you expect of her?"

Darcy had been delighted to find that Elizabeth loved books and was an avid reader of many different subjects. The ladies of the *ton* were so insipid, speaking only of the weather, fashions, or the latest *on-dit* that Darcy hesitated to speak at length with any of them. But, he looked forward to future discussions with Miss Elizabeth Bennet and, perhaps, even marriage to her should they prove compatible. He smiled as he thought he might even fall in love with her.

Bennet cleared his throat rather loudly recalling Darcy to the conversation at hand. "Mr. Darcy?"

With a sheepish smile, Darcy said, "My apologies, sir. What was your question again, please?"

"I asked what you would expect of my daughter if you contemplated a courtship."

The warmth of embarrassment seeped into his cheeks as Darcy had been woolgathering instead of paying close attention to the conversation.

Bennet, though, was hard pressed to maintain a frown. *This is most entertaining and getting better and better.*

With a stronger voice, Darcy said, "I would expect Miss Elizabeth to just be herself. I'm not like most men in wanting a wife that is mere decoration on my arm or just to bear my children. I want a companion to love, cherish, and protect. The mother of my children must be intelligent, loving, and kind caring for others as well. I have many tenants on my property in Derbyshire, and the mistress of Pemberley will be expected to do her part in caring for their needs as well."

Raising his hand, Mr. Bennet stopped Darcy's comments. "I assure you that my Lizzy would do very well as mistress of an estate. She helps me in regard to my own." Here, he stopped talking for a moment then continued ruefully. "Raising her like I would if I had had a son may have been a mistake. It has made her rather independent, more so than my other daughters." He now turned to Bingley. "You, sir, will find that Jane is more subdued in her personality than my Lizzy. But, perhaps, that is something you would prefer."

Bingley's face burned as he realized that Jane's father was far more discerning than he realized. And his mouth dropped open as it was impressed upon him that the next interrogation would be performed on him.

"And, Mr. Darcy, what would you offer my daughter?"

But Darcy never got the opportunity to answer Mr. Bennet as there was a knock at the door again, and it opened to reveal Elizabeth. Darcy's breath caught in his throat as his attraction strengthened for the young woman.

Immediately, Elizabeth curtseyed and welcomed the two men as they stood and bowed to her. "Good morning, Mr. Bingley…Mr. Darcy."

Mr. Bennet didn't miss the hesitation in her greeting and the light blush that graced her expressive face. He choked back his feelings and smiled at his favorite daughter. "Good morning, my dear. 'Tis a lovely day, is it not?"

Elizabeth's blush intensified as she took note that both men had to have come for her and Jane's sake. It left her rather speechless.

Before inviting her to sit, Bennet asked if Jane had also arisen.

"Yes, she has and will be down soon. Should I ask Hill to bring more refreshments for you and your visitors, Papa?"

"Are your mother and sisters awake yet?"

"No, you know how they are after a ball. We should not see them for another hour or more."

"So, I surmise these young men haven't come solely to get to know me better. When Jane comes down, ask Mrs. Hill to supply more refreshments to the main parlor and have Sarah join you as chaperone since your mother is not available."

"Yes, Papa." Smiling and curtseying again, Elizabeth exited her father's library. She found her heart galloping a bit after seeing Mr. Darcy. *Have they come to visit with Jane and me?* Stopping a moment at the mirror in the hallway, she checked to make sure her appearance was comely in spite of checking before she came down the stairs. However, her hands were shaking a little in excitement as she contemplated a gentleman seriously seeking her out. *And he is such a handsome gentleman as well.* This time she grinned.

Chapter V

Before arriving at the parlor, Elizabeth heard Jane descending the stairs and hurried to meet her.

"Jane! Jane! Guess who's come to call." Elizabeth whispered a little too loudly.

"You seem very excited about callers. I cannot begin to guess who is here."

"Mr. Darcy and Mr. Bingley."

"Oh." For a moment, Jane was speechless. Then she grinned as Elizabeth had and said, "We must welcome our guests."

"Yes, we must."

After the ball, when they had arrived home, the two young women had stayed up an hour longer talking about the evening and their dances with the newcomers. To have them arrive the next morning nearly caused the two sisters to swoon. They had been very impressed with the looks and deportment of Mr. Bingley and Mr. Darcy and had wondered if they would call. And now they were here, and Jane and Elizabeth were stricken with the giggles necessitating them ducking into the small parlor to avoid being seen and heard.

"Jane, we cannot loiter. Hill has already shown them to the large parlor. Mr. Darcy and Mr. Bingley will wonder where we got to." And the giggles took them away for a moment more before both put on a more serious mien although with smiles, smoothed their skirts, patted their hair, and declared each looked lovely. Then they headed to the larger parlor with nerves that felt like their mother's.

Upon the ladies' entry, Darcy and Bingley jumped to their feet and bowed to them receiving curtseys in return. All four had smiles of delight as the men took the hand of their favored lady and placed a kiss on the back. Both young women blushed as they were in their own home and were not wearing gloves to the delight of the two men whose kisses lingered for a moment longer than necessary. The morning was off to a rather good start.

Bingley assisted Jane to sit on a small settee and then seated himself beside her with a smile. "Miss Bennet, you look lovely this morning."

"May I assist you, Miss Elizabeth?" Darcy said and helped her to one of two chairs in a grouping at her nod. He also sat in an adjoining chair once she was seated.

"Thank you, Mr. Darcy. And are you well this fine day?"

"Yes, I am and even better now that you are here."

Elizabeth could feel her blush deepen as her face warmed, and she looked down with a smile. "Thank you, Mr. Darcy." But neither knew what to say after that. It was one of the few times in her life that her thoughts were so unorganized that Elizabeth found herself speechless.

However, that was not a problem with Jane and Mr. Bingley. With their heads together, they were softly conversing about the assembly and how fine it was.

Darcy and Elizabeth were relieved when Hill entered the parlor with coffee and refreshments and Sarah followed with the tea tray and sandwiches. She was glad that Jane was serving the drinks as she might have spilled them when pouring as nervous as she felt to have this man calling on her.

What did I do to deserve such a handsome man? No matter, he is here and we must converse.

"Mr. Darcy, we must enter into conversation. I assume you are a bit shy, but that is not usually part of my nature. I tend to be rather more amiable than I find myself today."

Darcy could not help but smile as his knowledge of French, because of his D'Arcy ancestry, was quite extensive. "Did you know, Miss Elizabeth, that the French term for amiable also means 'worthy to be loved,' and that even our English word has a secondary sense of 'exciting love or delight?'"

Elizabeth's mouth went dry, and her breath hitched. *My, my. He doesn't say much, but when he does...* She couldn't form a thought for a few moments as she looked down at her lap and smoothed her skirts. When she finally looked at him, she smiled and it was his turn to have a hitched breath as her eyes twinkled in mirth. "Mr. Darcy, if we continue with this topic, I shall be blushing to my toes."

Too late, Lizzy knew she had said too much and proceeded to turn bright red as Mr. Darcy grinned and pinked himself with even the tips of his ears darkening in color. Quickly he turned the conversation.

"What books do you enjoy, Miss Elizabeth?"

Softly breathing a sigh of relief, she cleared her throat. "Shakespeare's plays, I believe, are my favorites. I enjoy a number of poets' works also, especially Robbie Burns and William Wordsworth. There are many of the classics that appeal to me as well. But, most of all, I love a good novel. Mrs. Radcliffe writes some very exciting tales." With her eyes, Elizabeth dared him to deny her comment.

Darcy laughed and to her amazement said, "Yes, she does. I have three first editions of her writings in my library at Pemberley."

"You do?" said Elizabeth with wide-eyed amazement.

"Yes, I do. My sister and I both enjoy a leisurely evening with a good book."

"Oh, you have a sister? Is she close to your age?"

"No, Georgiana is nearly twelve years my junior. Since my father died, I have felt more like a father to her than her brother. My cousin, Richard Fitzwilliam, and I are her guardians."

For a moment, Elizabeth felt his pain, and she reached over and gently patted his hand. "I'm so sorry for your loss."

Darcy, in turn, was so moved by her gesture, he covered her hand with his other one then kissed the back of hers again causing her to shiver.

"Are you cold, Miss Elizabeth? Perhaps, I could stoke the fire. The days are still a little cool until spring is totally upon us."

Shaking her head, she smiled. "Thank you, sir, but I am fine."

Much to her chagrin, her mother appeared and loudly greeted both men who stood and bowed.

"Mr. Bingley...and Mr. Darcy. How nice of you to call." Dismissing Sarah to her duties, Mrs. Bennet rang for Hill and ordered fresh tea, coffee, and more sandwiches before seating herself. She, thereupon, dominated the remainder of the conversations as Jane and Lizzy grimaced at her loud voice and her determination to learn more about the young men who were pursuing her daughters. She had no thoughts that they would be doing otherwise. After all, she had five lovely daughters to supply with husbands. Her fear of living in the hedgerows when Mr. Bennet passed had given her an inordinate fear of that time as Longbourn was entailed to a cousin she had never met. But if she had been a betting woman, Mrs. Bennet would surmise that he would toss her and her girls off the estate upon inheriting it. Nothing could dissuade her of any other outcome.

Bingley and Darcy left shortly thereafter, promising Jane and Elizabeth they would call again, with Mrs. Bennet loudly proclaiming they were welcome to come any time and issuing an invitation to dine with the family two days hence, which the two men accepted. No one seemed to notice or to mind that they had stayed long past the normal visiting time. Darcy and Bingley, however, had determined that on the next visit, they would invite the girls for a walk...with a chaperone, of course. Propriety must be observed.

***

Riding back to Netherfield, both men agreed that Mrs. Bennet was a tiring, overbearing woman.

"Bingley, would we really want her as a mother-in-law?"

"Darcy, if Miss Bennet turns out to be the love of my life, yes, I would even accept her mother too. I find...I find that I'm totally captivated with Jane." Darcy frowned at the silly grin on his friend's face.

"But you will be only three miles from her should you marry. She would be at your home every day, I daresay," Darcy said with a shudder.

Bingley laughed. "And should you marry Miss Elizabeth, she would be *your* mother-in-law as well. What think you of that?"

"We would be two and a half days away in Derbyshire. 'Twould not bother me at all. I would have Elizabeth all to myself." Darcy grinned at the thought, and both young men laughed. Then the smiles vanished as they pondered the problem of Mrs. Bennet.

Thank You

Thank you so much for reading ***Elizabeth's Choice.*** I hope you derived as much enjoyment from reading it as I did in writing it.

I love Darcy and Elizabeth and all the other characters from Jane Austen's ***Pride and Prejudice.*** And I especially love writing about the courtship and marriage of our dear couple.

I hope to have another Pride and Prejudice variation before the end of the year. So, please join my mailing list by emailing me at Gianna@GiannaThomasAuthor.com, and I'll keep you posted and share with you some of the scenes prior to publication. I send only one email or less per week.

And now a favor, please. Reviews are very important to indie authors like me, so I ask you for an honest review of ***Darcy vs Bingley***. Please post your review on Amazon and/or Goodreads.

Please also share your thoughts and impressions of my books on my Facebook Fan page at **https://www.facebook.com/GiannaThomasAuthor/**. I would appreciate it if you would 'Like' my page as well. Thank you.

Other Books by Gianna Thomas

You can read about Gianna's other **Pride and Prejudice** variations in her **Darcy and Elizabeth** Series, as well as her other **Regency** romances in **The Four Lords' Saga** Series, available as eBooks and in paperback at Amazon locations worldwide. https://www.amazon.com/author/giannathomas.

And please follow Gianna on her Facebook page. **https://www.facebook.com/GiannaThomasAuthor/**

About the Author

Although a writer of sweet+ Regency romance, Gianna Thomas, a native Texan, doesn't hesitate to tackle some of the grittier events in life. Even back in Regency times, the world of that day experienced war, hatred, prejudice, and crimes against women. And, we even see those things today. It seems that people don't change. Romance, especially Regency romance, really appeals to Gianna, and she loves writing about it whether Pride and Prejudice variations with Darcy and Elizabeth or love stories involving dukes and duchesses. And she is a prolific reader of Regency romance as well.

Gianna discovered ***Pride and Prejudice***, and its many variations, what ifs and fan fiction. She was totally fascinated by the variety of plots that eager authors had utilized. After reading nearly 400 variations and fan fictions, Gianna now had P&P plots running through her head. She finally decided that they needed to be put to paper (today, on the computer), to see how they would develop. She had an absolute ball in writing about Darcy and Elizabeth and was pleased with how things developed. Her goal will always be to entertain and touch hearts. Hopefully, with her first rendering, ***Pride and Prejudice: Darcy Chooses***, she achieved that goal.

More recently, Gianna started looking beyond *Pride and Prejudice*, with her first foray into Regency Romance generally, with *The Four Lords' Saga* Series. She is finding that she loves all the lords, their ladies, and their families, and writing about them is one of the most fun-filled adventures she's ever been on. There are four books in the initial series, then there will be other novellas/short stories concerning the lords and their families. There's nothing better than to read and write about handsome bad boys who change their wicked ways for their ladies. And the four lords fit the bill perfectly. Join the many who will learn why four confirmed bachelors decide, unexpectedly, to seriously consider marriage after escaping parson's mousetrap for years. You will love the reason why.

And for P&P fans, never fear. There will be more Darcy and Elizabeth as well, mostly in the form of novellas and short stories.

Gianna Thomas is a former ghostwriter of poetry and e-books who became a widow after twenty-two years with her very own Mr. Darcy, who was her second husband. She lives a quiet life in a small Texas town with her cats and loves to read the many variations done by other lovers of *Pride and Prejudice* and Regency Romance.

Learn more about Gianna and her Regency Romance writings on her page at Amazon Author Central at **https://www.amazon.com/author/giannathomas**.

Also, please visit with her on Facebook at **https://www.facebook.com/GiannaThomasAuthor**/ And please Like her page.

Printed in Great Britain
by Amazon